# ITALIAN RENAISSANCE

# ILLUMINATIONS

# ITALIAN RENAISSANCE ILLUMINATIONS

## J. J. G. ALEXANDER

1977

CHATTO & WINDUS

LONDON

*To Mary*

First Published in the UK
in 1977 by Chatto & Windus Ltd.,
London

© J. J. G. Alexander 1977

ISBN 0 7011 2270 6

Printed in Switzerland by
IMPRIMERIES REUNIES

# Contents

# *Acknowledgements*

The author and publishers would like to express their sincere thanks to the following institutions and individuals who kindly provided materials and granted permission to reproduce them in this volume.

*Color Plates*

FLORENCE, Biblioteca Medicea Laurenziana, Plates 3a, 3b, 4, 5 (Photo, Dr. G. B. Pineider, Florence).

FLORENCE, Biblioteca Nazionale Centrale di Firenze, Plates 11, 12 (Photo, Guido Sansoni, Florence).

FLORENCE, Biblioteca Riccardiana, Plates 1, 2 (Photo, Dr. G. B. Pineider, Florence).

KASSEL, Landesbibliothek u. Murhardsche Bibliothek der Stadt Kassel, Plate 40 (Photo, Werner Lengemann, Kassel).

LONDON, Reproduced by permission of the British Library Board,
Plates 6, 7, 38, 39.

MILAN, Archivio Storico e Biblioteca Trivulziana (Castello Sforzesco), Plates 29, 30, 31, 32 (Photo, Comune di Milano Archivio Fotografico dei Civici Musei).

MODENA, Biblioteca Estense, Plates 19, 20, 21, 22, 27a, 27b, 28 (Photo, Fotografia Editrice Cav. Uff. Umberto Orlandini, Modena).

NEW YORK, The Pierpont Morgan Library, Plates 17, 18.

PARIS, Bibliothèque Nationale, Plates 8, 9, 10, 13, 14 (Photo, Bibliothèque Nationale, Paris).

ROME, Biblioteca Apostolica Vaticana, Plates 23, 24, 25, 26.

VIENNA, Österreichische Nationalbibliothek, Plates 15, 16, 33, 34, 35, 36, 37.

*Black-and-White Figures*

CESENA, Biblioteca Malatestiana, Figure XIX (Photo, Tanya Vinogradoff).

FLORENCE, Biblioteca Medicea Laurenziana, Figure VII (Photo, Dr. G. B. Pineider, Florence).

FLORENCE, Museo San Marco, Figure VI (Photo, Gabinetto Fotografico, Sopr. Gallerie, Florence).

GLASGOW, University Library, Figures X, XI.

LONDON, Reproduced by permission of the British Library Board, Figures XIV, XVI.

MODENA, Biblioteca Estense, Figure XII (Photo, Fotografia Editrice Cav. Uff. Umberto Orlandini, Modena).

NEW YORK, The Pierpont Morgan Library, Figure I.

OXFORD, Courtesy of the Curators of the Bodleian Library, Figures III, IV, V, IX, XVII.

PARIS, Bibliothèque Nationale, Figure VIII (Photo, Bibliothèque Nationale, Paris).

ROME, Biblioteca Apostolica Vaticana, Figure XIII.

SIENA, Libreria Piccolomini, Figure XV (Photo, Fratelli Alinari, Florence).

VENICE, Biblioteca Marciana, Figure II (Photo, Foto Toso, Venice).

WASHINGTON, Library of Congress Rosenwald Collection, Figure XVIII.

# Introduction

Italian Renaissance illumination is inevitably overshadowed by the great works of contemporary Italian monumental painting. Its comparative neglect is also, however, a matter of a change of taste brought about in the course of the nineteenth century as a result of the Gothic Revival. This is clear from the fact that in the early nineteenth century the most admired illuminator was Giulio Clovio (1498–1578), whom Vasari called "the Michelangelo in miniature of our day." Today the Book of Kells, the Winchester Bible, or the *Très Riches Heures* of Jean de Berry are likely to be better known to more people than any work of Clovio's (Figure I).[1] But although manuscript illumination is now particularly associated with the Middle Ages, it continued to be a vital and creative form of art in Italy in the fifteenth and sixteenth centuries. Its eventual decline can be attributed more to the invention of printing and the attendant changes in the production of books, especially, of course, in mechanical methods of illustration by woodcut, than to any other single cause.

What will distinguish the examples chosen here from earlier Italian illumination? In what sense can they be considered typical products of the cultural movement in Italy known as the Renaissance? A first and obvious point is the question of the texts. The interest in all aspects of Greek and Roman antiquity, which, although it had started much earlier, above all with Petrarch (1304–74), became so widespread and so vital a factor in fifteenth-century Italy, resulted in a renewed demand for classical texts, both those already known and others only just discovered by the humanists. Finely written and richly illuminated copies of the works of such Latin authors as Virgil (Plates 1–2), Suetonius (Plates 13–14), Cicero (Plates 33–34), and many others were produced in huge numbers. As the century progressed, this interest was expanded to include Greek authors such as Aristotle or Homer in the original, not just in Latin translation (Plates 35–37).

Secondly, this expansion of book production and the choice of texts to be copied was the consequence of a new manner of patronage. In the earlier Middle Ages, the main producers of manuscripts were the monastic com-

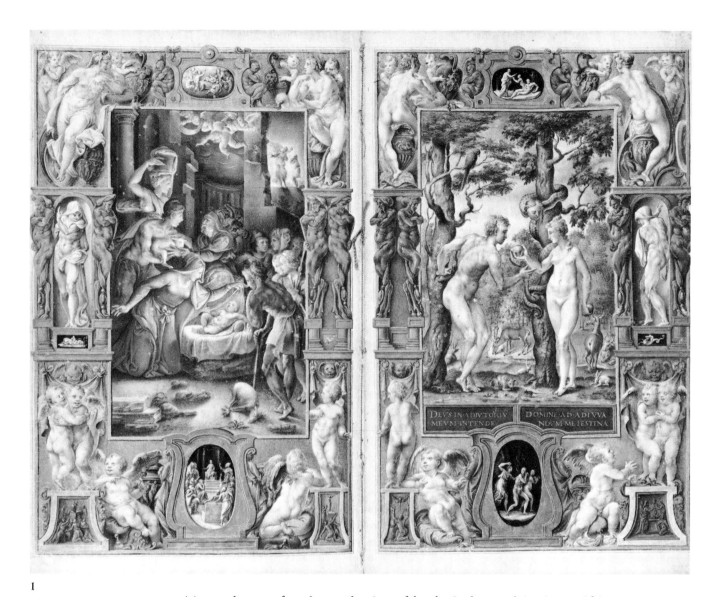

I

munities, and even after the production of books had passed in the twelfth to thirteenth centuries to predominantly lay professionals, especially those working in the University cities, the majority of the texts continued to be religious. Similarly, the great collections of manuscripts belonged to religious establishments, whether monasteries or cathedrals. Up to this time only richer ecclesiastics, or royalty, or the higher nobility were likely to own books. By the fourteenth century it had become more common for private people including laymen to own books, but still in not very large quantities. The libraries formed by Charles V, King of France (1337–1380), and his Valois brothers, above all Jean de Berry (d. 1416), were quite exceptional in their size and splendor, and the French Royal Library was also of primary importance in that it was to become, in spite of many vicissitudes, a permanent institution. It was housed at first by Charles V in the Palais du Louvre, and the number of its volumes was increased by successive Kings of France. It was also available to scholars who wished to consult its many manuscripts.

In Italy we see the same thing happening during that period or a little later, especially in Milan, where the Visconti rulers began to establish a library —an inventory in 1426 already listing nine hundred and eighty-eight items. This had grown to a total of over a thousand volumes in 1499 when finally seized by the French at Pavia, a large part being removed by Louis XII to the Chateau of Blois. Over three hundred and eighty volumes from the Visconti library remain together in the Bibliothèque Nationale in Paris.[2] The political fragmentation and, at the same time, the substantial and increasing material prosperity of Italy were to result in the formation of a large number of private libraries, not only by the greater and lesser rulers of the various states, but also by individual wealthy merchants, such as Francesco Sassetti, partner in the Medici bank, and Filippo Strozzi,[3] as well as by various humanist scholars. The most important of the libraries formed at this time were those of the Visconti/ Sforza, Dukes of Milan, already mentioned; of the Medici in Florence; of the Aragonese rulers of Naples; of the D'Este in Ferrara; of the Gonzaga in Mantua; and of Federigo da Montefeltro, Duke of Urbino. Successive Popes, particularly Eugenius IV, Nicholas V, Pius II, and Paul II, were also considerable collectors and patrons in their own right, but it was not until Sixtus IV (1471–84) that a Vatican Library was built and a permanent librarian, Bartolomeo Platina, appointed.[4] Several of the Cardinals formed important libraries, notably Bessarion (d. 1472) who finally bequeathed his manuscripts to the city of Venice, so that many of them are today in the Biblioteca Marciana. The more powerful and wealthier rulers generally employed their own scribes and illuminators, as well as commissioning books from the booksellers. At the same time the professional booksellers (*cartolaii*) were increasing in number to meet the demand of the humanist scholars and their pupils for books. We are particularly well informed about the activities of the Florentine *cartolaio* Vespasiano de Bisticci, from his own writings.[5] He was especially proud of the part he played in supplying books for the library collected by Federigo da Montefeltro, most of which is now housed in the Vatican Library. Vespasiano's comment that all the Duke's books were handwritten manuscripts, and that the Duke would have been ashamed to own a printed book, is well known.

If we look at the manuscripts themselves, we will find that many of them are distinguishable from both earlier Italian and contemporary Northern manuscripts by the type of script and decoration used. The new type of script was developed by the same humanist scholars who were instrumental in the discovery of many new classical texts, as well as in correcting and revising well-known ones. Referred to now as "humanist script," it is familiar to us because it was used by the earliest printers in Italy for many of their books (hence "roman" type-face) and has gradually replaced all other forms of the printed and written Western alphabet.

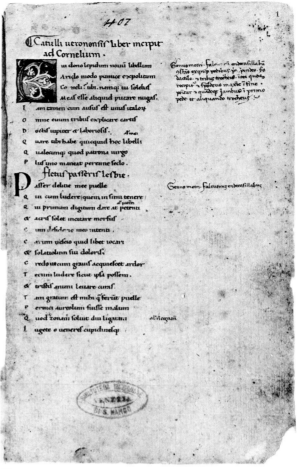

II

Both script and decoration were based on earlier models of the Romanesque period, in the eleventh to twelfth centuries, which in turn were derived from Carolingian innovations of the ninth century.[6] The form of decoration familiarly known as "white-vine," or in Italian *bianchi girari,* is based on the initial decoration of eleventh to twelfth-century central Italian manuscripts. The decorators of these volumes had adopted the schematized foliage scroll used in late ninth-century Carolingian manuscripts, particularly those from Saint Gall, and in tenth-century Ottonian manuscripts from southern Germany. Probably the earliest example of the use of the revived white-vine initial is in a volume of Catullus which is also probably the first manuscript to be written in humanist script by Poggio Bracciolini in Florence in the years 1400–02 (Figure II).[7] A notable feature of these early humanist initials is the way the scroll —a more or less inorganic stem with flattened nodes, trilobes and palmettes— is left uncolored and unshaded on a roughly square ground, which is particolored in contrasting colors such as red, blue, green or yellow. How close the initials are to earlier Tuscan, Umbrian, and Roman manuscripts can be seen from a comparison of an initial *V* from a copy of Saint Gregory's *Dialogues* probably made in the region of Rome c. 1125 (Figure IV) with an initial *O* (Figure III) in a copy of Cicero's *De Oratore* finished at Florence by an

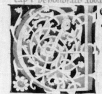

III                    IV

unknown scribe on January 13, 1412 (Florentine style).[8] When Leonardo Bruni sent a manuscript of Cicero to Niccolo Niccoli in 1407 he asked that it be decorated *vetusto more*, "in the ancient manner,"[9] and that historicism indicates a new attitude toward the past. This type of initial quickly became standard in humanist texts and was adopted with regional variations all over Italy. The *bianchi girari* also came to be used in border decorations, and another specifically Italian feature is the introduction of classical nude *putti* into the scroll. These occur especially as supporters for the owners' coat-of-arms in the lower margin as in the classical *imago clipeata*. The white-vine scroll was soon combined with more naturalistic plant forms, and small scenes were inserted in roundels in the borders, showing portrait heads, studies of animals, birds, insects, etc., as can be seen in a Cicero with illumination attributed to Francesco d'Antonio del Cherico, the leading illuminator in Florence until his death in 1484 (Figure V).[10] This form of decoration is specifically a feature of Italian Renaissance illumination; it is rarely found elsewhere, and only then as a result of Italian influence.

By this time, book illumination in Italy was no longer a major innovative art, and the main developments were dictated by the architects, sculptors, and monumental painters. Book illuminators tended to follow closely the style of their

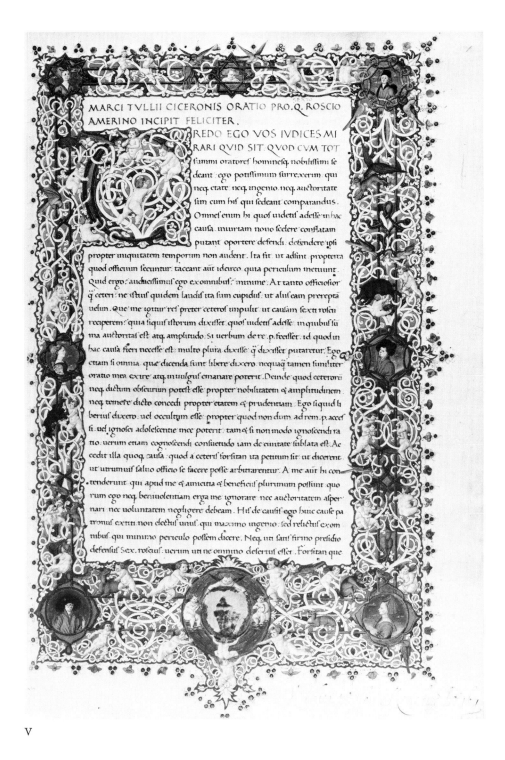

V

great contemporaries and to copy their compositions. In this sense too, therefore, much of fifteenth-century illumination is typical of the Renaissance in that it adopts a particular language of forms, especially in its depiction of space by the use of vanishing point perspective; in its preoccupation with human anatomy, particularly the nude (Plate 6); and in its debts to classical art. Quite a number of artists who worked also or mainly as fresco or panel painters executed miniatures as well—examples being Pisanello, Fra Angelico (Figure VI), Marco

Zoppo (Figure VIII),[11] Giovanni di Paolo (Plate 7), and Girolamo da Cremona (Plates 11–12).

We can contrast an initial *N* by Angelico, or at least from his workshop, with an initial *I* attributed to Lorenzo Monaco (the leading painter of the International Gothic style in Florence until his death c. 1422–24), who also exerted considerable influence on the young Angelico (born c. 1400–02). In the *I* (Figure VII) the prophet is, as it were, sandwiched between the upright of the initial and its background. Space is constructed in layers, and the figure is still a variation on the Gothic theme of the column statue. In the *N* (Figure VI), Saint Peter is shown as a monumental figure standing firmly in space and quite independent of the initial.

Lorenzo Monaco was a monk of the Monastery of the Angeli in Florence, and in the decoration of this initial, we see the large lush leaves, the cornflowers, and the bushy-tailed birds which are typical not only of the manuscripts produced in the Angeli, but of Florentine religious manuscripts in general during the first half of the fifteenth century.[12] Religious manuscripts continue to be decorated in this style deriving from earlier Gothic manuscript border decoration, just as they continue to be written in Gothic script. In the mid-fifteenth century, however, the two types of borders begin to be intermixed, and in the

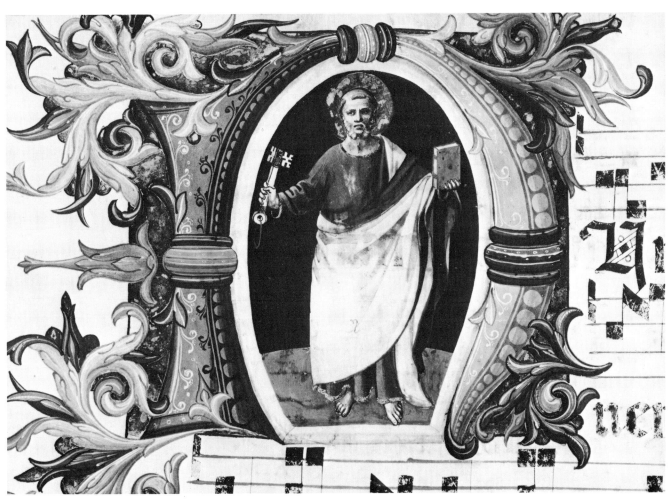

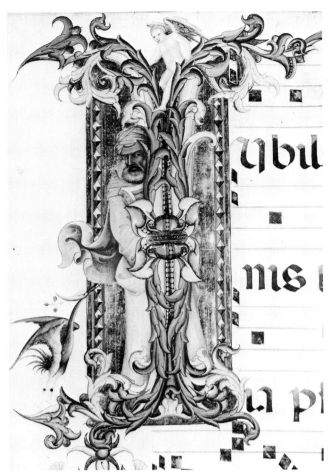

VII

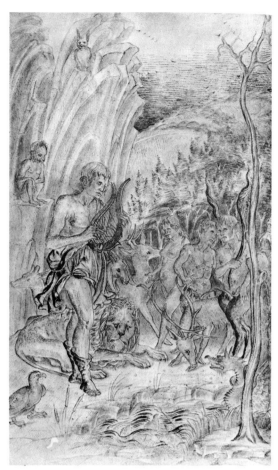

VIII

later fifteenth century the white-vine border tends to disappear. A mixture of fruit, flower, and foliage forms, *putti,* and classical and Renaissance architectural and sculptural motifs, such as cornucopiae and candelabra, can be seen, for example, in the Book of Hours illuminated in 1485, probably for Lorenzo dei Medici (Plates 3a, b). Not only the classical decorative details, but the way the Annunciation takes place in a portico, with views through to an extensive landscape on the left and the Virgin's bedchamber on the right, show that the artist was thinking of the scene as represented by contemporary painters. We know that the Florentines Gherardo and Monte di Miniato, who were mainly stationers and illuminators and who illuminated the magnificent Bible of Matthias Corvinus, King of Hungary (Plates 4–5), collaborated with Domenico Ghirlandaio (c. 1448–94) on a project in the Duomo in Florence. Their style clearly shows the influence of his work.

The lack of political unification in Italy is also reflected in the recognizable regional styles of illumination, although there are, naturally, numerous crosscurrents of influences, since artists frequently travelled to work on commissions in different centers. Milan, having close political, trading and cultural ties with Northern Europe, is one of the areas in Italy most influenced by Northern Gothic art. Numerous foreign artists came to work on the completion of the Cathedral, and in the late fourteenth and early fifteenth centuries Giovanni dei

Grassi and Michelino da Besozzo were also important due to their influence in the reverse direction as far afield as Bohemia and England.[13] The stylistic tradition they established proved strong and enduring, and the leading illuminator in Milan in the 1430s, the so-called "Master of the *Vitae Imperatorium*," continued to use a Gothic drapery and figure style and Gothic-type border decoration.[14] Even such white-vine decoration as there is in Milan involved a more Gothic type of scroll. In the later fifteenth century outside influences were felt, first from the east in the work of Mantegna, which influenced such painters as Foppa, and later, from Florence with the arrival of Leonardo himself in 1482–83. The miniatures of the young Maximilian Sforza's schoolbook (Plates 29–32) not only give a vivid idea of the schooling of a Renaissance prince, but the portraits of Maximilian and Lodovico il Moro reflect the style, may even be by the hand of the court portraitist, Ambrogio de Predis, with whom Leonardo stayed in Milan.

In the Veneto too, the transition to a specifically Renaissance style of book illumination was only gradual. The leading illuminator of the earlier fifteenth century, Cristoforo Cortese, developed his style from the dominant school of illumination in the northeast in the fourteenth century, that of Bologna.[15] The change, when it came, was from Padua where the presence of the University

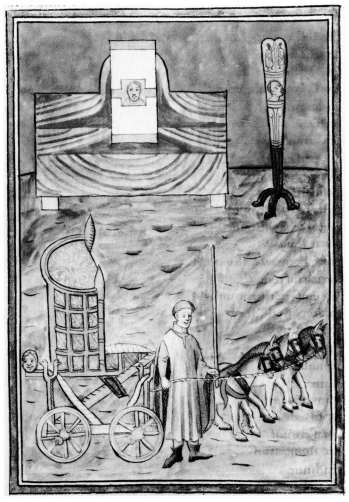

and a circle of antiquarians interested in the collection and study of Roman remains was crucial. Already in 1436 the bishop of Padua, Pietro Donato, being at Basel for the Council, took the opportunity to have a copy made of a Carolingian manuscript preserved in the chapter library at Speyer. This copy, since lost, contained various texts connected with the administration of the Late Roman Empire, particularly the list of officials known as the *Notitia Dignitatum,* and it was illustrated with a series of miniatures accurately copying an original of probably the early fifth century (Figure IX).[16] Donato employed an artist who happened to be available locally, a Frenchman, Perronet Lamy, but again this is an example of a new humanist historicism, for these were careful copies wherein the artist must have been instructed to remain as close as possible to the originals, even if he could not always resist the temptation to alter and embellish.

In Donato's manuscript is contained a note written by an inexhaustibly curious and energetic antiquary and traveller, Ciriaco d'Ancona, who visited not only Constantinople but Greece, and even drew the sculptures on the Parthenon.[17] Ciriaco, in turn, infected a younger scholar, Felice Feliciano of Verona, with his enthusiasm for inscriptions and classical remains.[18] In the year 1464 an outing on Lake Garda was arranged to record inscriptions in which Felice was joined by two other antiquaries, Samuele da Tradate and Giovanni Marcanova, and as a fourth no less a person than Andrea Mantegna. This combination of the interests of the antiquaries and the artistic influence of Mantegna was to have a very great impact on manuscript illumination.

Marcanova's own antiquarian collection of inscriptions, started at Padua and finished at Bologna, exists in various copies, one of which was planned for presentation to Malatesta Novello of Cesena. The presentation copy is probably the manuscript in Modena, completed on October 1, 1465, though it seems that Malatesta Novello died before he could receive it. It is largely written and illustrated by Felice and shows the same passion for the recording but also for the reconstruction of the classical past (Figure XII).

We can see the process at work if we compare the white-vine decoration of the Florentine Cicero decorated by Francesco d'Antonio (Figure V) with a Suetonius of the Paduan school (Plates 13–14). Whereas the Florentine humanists had adopted a form of decoration which, as it happened, was northern and medieval in origin, the Paduans concocted a medley of genuine classical motifs to make a pastiche, which, though it does not resemble anything that would ever have been found in any actual classical roll or codex, nevertheless is apposite and learned. For example, each life of each Emperor is prefaced by representations of coins which he issued. Another antiquarian practice found in these manuscripts is the use of parchment stained green or purple, as in Late

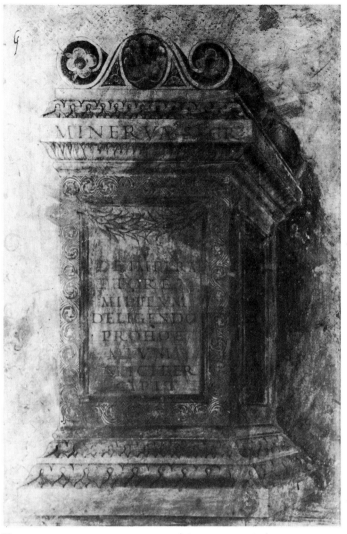

X

Antique luxury *codices*. This is seen, for example, in the Virgil with miniatures by Marco Zoppo made for a member of the Venetian Morosini family c. 1470 (Figure VIII).

The other important innovation of the Paduan school was to treat the frontispiece or title page of the manuscript as if it were an actual classical inscribed stone monument. Some early examples occur in manuscripts written and decorated by Felice himself (Figures X–XI), and there are others in a group of classical and humanistic texts copied in Padua for the Englishman, John Tiptoft, earl of Worcester, who was studying at the University in 1458/9.[19] They gradually become more elaborate (Figure XVI, Plates 20–21), until the whole of a page of script is placed in front of a sort of monumental arch forming an "antique architectural gateway into the book" (Plates 17–18), as Professor Mitchell has expressed it.[20] Many of the early printed books, especially those from the press of Nicholas Jenson, have hand-illuminated decoration of this kind.[21] The idea was later taken over in printed books with wood-

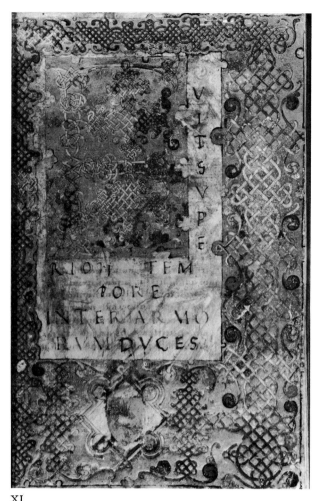

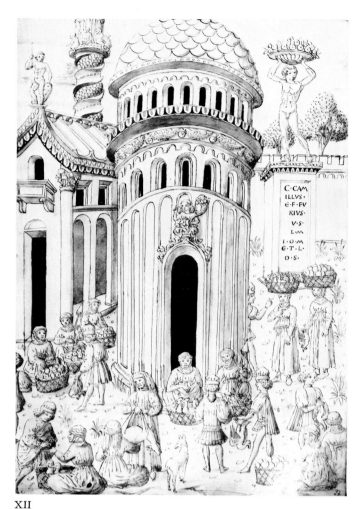

XI

XII

cut title-pages and lies behind a whole series of imaginative and fantastic designs.

If the earliest examples of the new antiquarian style of illumination came from northeast Italy, the style quickly spread elsewhere. A major illuminator whose style was greatly indebted to Mantegna seems to have moved to Rome where he worked for Cardinal Francesco Gonzaga (Figure XIII, Plates 13–14). Often he worked in manuscripts written by one of the great calligraphers of the Renaissance, Bartolomeo Sanvito, who himself also came from Padua and later returned there. Sanvito used epigraphic capitals based on early Imperial Roman inscriptions, and significantly he wrote a number of copies of the collections of inscriptions made by another important antiquary, Fra Giocondo of Verona. These too are decorated in the Paduan style, possibly by Sanvito himself.[22]

Mantegna's influence extended also to Venice, where an illuminator now identifiable from documented works as Leonardo Bellini, son of Jacopo, and thus brother of Giovanni and Gentile Bellini and brother-in-law of Mantegna, was active (Figure XIV).[23] It is not always clear whether artists were working in Padua or Venice, since they might execute commissions for patrons in both places. An example is the so-called *Maestro dei Putti* who seems to have been employed especially by the printer Nicholas Jenson for the decoration of special copies printed on vellum, again with classical antiquarian motifs often in tinted ink drawings, but who also illuminated manuscripts (Plates 15–16). Leonardo Bellini, though his figures and his rocky landscapes show the influence of Mantegna, continued to use a Gothic flower-spray type of border, for instance in the copies of official state documents of the Republic, the *Promissiones* of the Doges on taking office, the *Comissiones* of the Procurators of Saint Mark, and the instructions for the Governors appointed to the various cities of the *terra firma,* as well as the captains of the galleys sent to Flanders each year. It is interesting that in Venice with its thriving printing industry these documents continued to be written and illuminated by hand until at least the end of the sixteenth century.

It has been suggested that Mantegna himself illuminated a small manuscript which is today in Paris (Plates 8–10). He also knew and certainly influenced another outstanding illuminator, Girolamo da Cremona, to whom Barbara of Brandenburg, Marchesa of Mantua, gave the commission, to be arranged by Mantegna, for the completion of a Missal (still in Mantua) in 1461. Significantly,

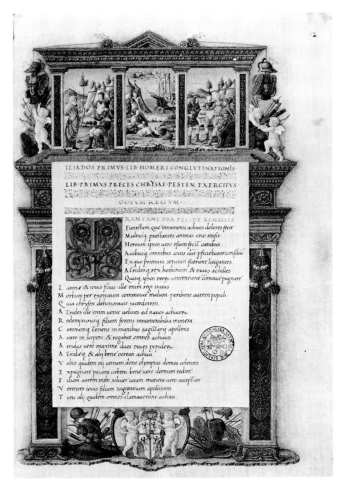

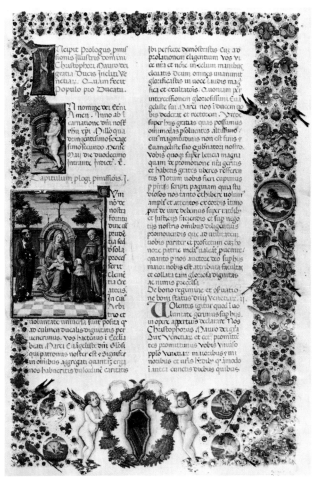

XIII

XIV

Girolamo was required to replace a Lombard artist, Belbello da Pavia, whose still essentially Gothic style evidently no longer gave satisfaction.[24] Girolamo was one of the most talented and successful of Italian fifteenth-century illuminators. From Mantua he was called to Siena to work on the Choir Books of the Cathedral, which today are exhibited in the Piccolimini Library.[25] The miniatures and historiated initials in these huge volumes are the equivalent of small panel paintings and are symptomatic of the Italian artist's constant tendency to express himself on a monumental scale. Although sometimes found elsewhere in Europe, such *corali* are an especially common type of illuminated book in Italy. In fact every great monastic and cathedral church seems to have had sets of antiphonals and graduals on this grand scale. Their text and the musical notation had to be written large enough to be seen at a good distance by the choir gathered round the lectern. Not only are they of great size, but they also had heavy bindings of wooden boards with metal ornaments to protect them. During the Napoleonic wars in Italy, with the resultant secularization of much church property, many such establishments were looted, and it is not surprising that these books should have been mutilated and the miniatures cut out. Just at this time collectors were beginning to appreciate their value, and many cuttings, often bearing optimistic ascriptions of their earlier owners to Giotto, Angelico, Mantegna, or other masters, have found their way into museums, print rooms and libraries all over the world.

Girolamo worked with a number of other artists on the Siena *corali,* the most gifted of his colleagues being Liberale da Verona (Figure XV). The two artists evidently influenced each other and, where the payments are not clear, it is not always easy to decide who is responsible for a particular miniature. In fact they may have collaborated on the same page. From Siena, Girolamo went to Florence where he executed the illustrations of a *de luxe* alchemical manuscript (Plates 11–12) and collaborated on a Breviary for Sta. Maria Nuova with Gherardo di Miniato, for which Gherardo received payment in 1477. Girolamo's type of border with gold chiaroscuro scrolls, simulated jewels, cameos, and pearls was imitated by Florentine artists. It often replaced the type of white-vine or flower border used earlier by Francesco d'Antonio and others, for example in manuscripts illuminated by Monte and Gherardo di Miniato (Plates 4–5), by Boccardino, and by Attavante. Finally Girolamo seems to have returned to Venice, and the illumination of certain important Venetian printed books has been attributed to him (Plates 17–18).

In Naples, the first of the Aragonese Kings, Alfonso V (1401–58), after his final defeat of René of Anjou in 1442, began to amass a great library of manuscripts, which was increased by his successors. We have a series of catalogues drawn up by the royal librarians and numerous records of payments

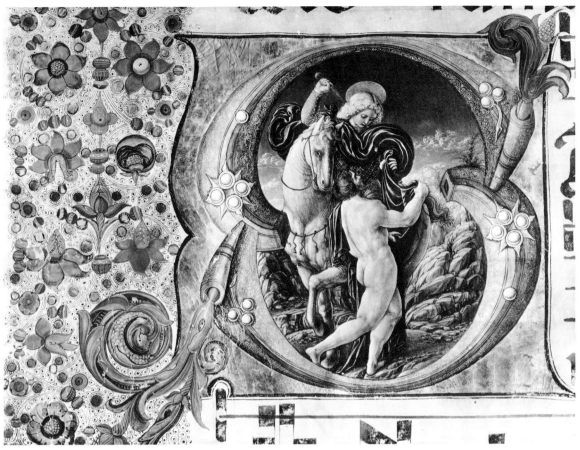

XV

in the royal accounts to both scribes and illuminators, and thanks to the fine volumes of Tammaro di Marinis we can build up an unusually full picture of the Naples royal library.[26] The influence of Northern, especially Franco-Flemish, styles of illumination is strong in many of the manuscripts, as can be seen in the very Gothic frontispiece of Alfonso riding on horseback like a medieval knight in his copy of Vegetius, *de re militari* (Figure XVII and contrast Plate 33). This is to be explained partly as a legacy of the Anjou rulers (René of Anjou had finally to leave Italy after his attempt to capture and to hold the Kingdom had failed, Plates 8–10), partly by the indirect influence of Northern Gothic style via Spanish illumination, and partly by the presence of a number of Northern artists. The latter included a prolific scribe and illuminator, Gioacchino de Gigantibus, whose father came from Nuremburg.[27] He had evidently learnt the type of white-vine decoration which he used in Florence. He then worked in Rome for Pius II and others, and finally came to Naples. Another artist, Niccola Rapicano, uses flower-spray borders of Flemish type but inserts into them nude *putti*. At the same time his miniature of Ferdinand of Aragon on horseback (Plate 33, contrast Figure XVII) takes up one of the great Renaissance themes, the equestrian monument. The Paduan antiquarian style of illumination, which, as has been said, spreads to Rome in the 1470s, also penetrates to Naples, and many of the manuscripts show a regional variation

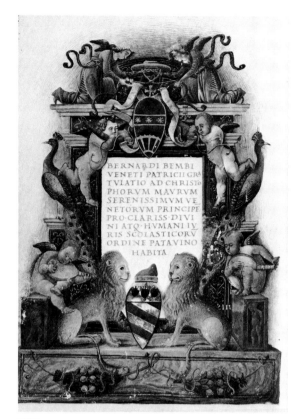

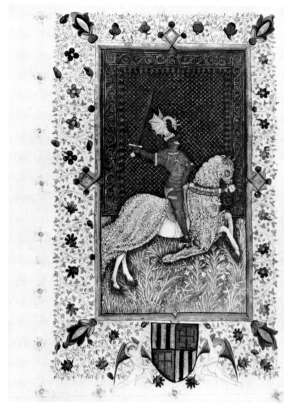

on the idea of the triumphal arch frontispiece (Plates 35–37). An illuminator
known to have worked in this style, Gasparo Romano, is perhaps the illuminator
of a Horace whose frontispiece of this type bears the Naples Royal arms.[28]

The library of Federigo da Montefeltro, Duke of Urbino, was built up
partly with the help of Vespasiano da Bisticci in Florence as has been mentioned.
Thus the Bible in two volumes (Vat. Urb. Lat. 1–2) ordered in 1476 was
illuminated in the workshop of the Florentine illuminator Attavante dei Atta-
vanti (1452–c. 1520).[29] Other manuscripts, such as the Duke's Dante (Plates
23–26), are illuminated by Ferrarese artists. The D'Este court at Ferrara under
Niccolo III, Lionello, and Borso d'Este was a major center for book illumination. All three rulers were notable patrons, and not only Italian artists such as
Pisanello, Jacopo Bellini, and Piero della Francesca, but also the Netherlandish painter Roger van der Weyden came to work in Ferrara. Borso d'Este
(1450–71) commissioned a great Bible for his own library in 1455 (Plates
19–22), in which a number of illuminators had a hand. Evidently the senior of
these was Taddeo Crivelli, who came from Lombardy, as is clear, for example,
in the landscape conventions he uses (Plate 19). The flower borders of the
Bible are notable for their exquisite filigree work, and there are also beautiful
red and blue penwork borders and initials. Characteristic of Ferrarese manuscripts are the roundels with nature studies reminiscent of Pisanello, such as
deer, birds of prey, etc. The use of gold in ornamental patterns of amazing
intricacy is extraordinarily lavish and the production of these Bibles (another

was commissioned for use in the Certosa of San Cristoforo) on such a scale is a strange harking back to the Romanesque period, when all the great monasteries had giant Bibles for reading in their refectories. It is right to remember that even in a humanistic court in the middle of the fifteenth century, the first book to be ordered for the library and entered in the catalogue was still a copy of the Holy Scriptures.

A large number of artists worked on the Bible under Crivelli's direction, among them Franco dei Russi—who worked later in Urbino for Federigo da Montefeltro (Plate 26), and in Venice, where he experimented with the architectural frontispiece (Figure XVI)[30]—and Giorgio d'Alemagna (Plate 21). The latter's son, Tommaso da Modena, is one of the leading illuminators of the next generation in Ferrara, although he too worked elsewhere, at Bologna for example. The second D'Este Bible, that of the Certosa, was mainly illuminated by Guglielmo Giraldi, who among many other commissions worked on the Dante for Federigo da Montefeltro, whose miniatures were never completed (Plates 23–25). The influence of the expressionistic style of the contemporary Ferrarese painters Ercole dei Roberti and Cosimo Tura on these illuminators is clear.

Enough has been said to give an idea of the quantity and quality of Italian Renaissance illumination up to c. 1500, the chronological limit taken for this selection. This is, of course, an arbitrary limitation of the material, since much

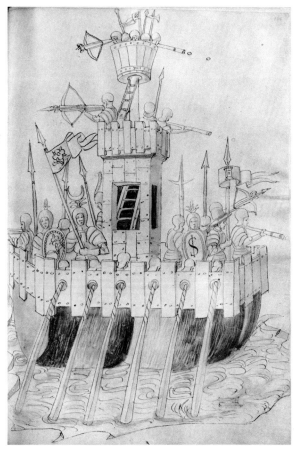

XVIII

of great importance survives from the early sixteenth century. Many equally fine manuscripts have been passed over and, in particular, certain classes of illumination are not properly represented, especially the scientific and pseudo-scientific texts, whether medical, botanical, astronomical or astrological, and the treatises on warfare, such as Valturius' *De re militari* written for Sigismondo Malatesta of Rimini, of which there were a number of fine illustrated manuscripts (Figure XVIII), as well as one of the earliest printed editions fully illustrated with woodcuts.[31] Another text, finely illuminated copies of which were common in the Renaissance, is Petrarch's *Trionfi,* here only represented by one example—though a magnificent one—the Cassel manuscript illuminated by Marmitta of Parma (Plate 40).[32]

Moreover, there were many other regional centers of lesser importance than those discussed, but also producing illuminated manuscripts—places such as Bologna, Brescia, Genoa and Cesena. The latter has the most perfect of surviving Renaissance libraries, built to the design of Matteo Nuti for Malatesta Novello between 1447 and 1452. The manuscripts for which he employed a series of copyists and illuminators, (the payments to whom with their respective shares of the work all having been recorded), remain miraculously intact as a collection. The contents of the library were commandeered by the French in the Napoleonic wars and transported to Paris, but all except two volumes were restored after the Peace of Vienna. This selection may therefore fittingly end with a picture (Figure XIX) of the sort of home for which many of these manuscripts were intended, in this case a chained library with stringent safeguards to ensure their safety.[33]

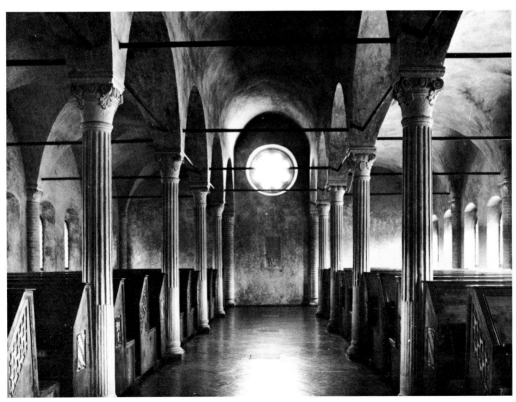

XIX

# Footnotes

1. For the admiration of Clovio see A.N.L. Munby, *Connoisseurs and Medieval Miniatures 1750–1850.* Oxford 1972, pp. 25 ff. The Hours of Cardinal Farnese, on which Vasari tells us Clovio worked for nine years, is now reproduced in facsimile, W. Smith, *The Farnese Hours.* New York 1976.

2. E. Pellegrin, *La bibliothèque des Visconti et des Sforza.* Paris 1955.

3. For Sassetti's library and the activities of the humanist Bartolomeo Fonzio while employed as his librarian, see A.C. de la Mare, "The library of Francesco Sassetti," *Essays in honour of Paul Oskar Kristeller,* ed. C.H. Clough. Manchester 1976.

4. J. Ruysschaert, "Miniaturistes 'romains' sous Pie II," *Enea Sivio Piccolomini. Papa Pio II.* Siena 1968.

5. Vespasiano da Bisticci, *Le Vite,* ed. A. Greco. Florence 1970. "(I libri) tutti iscritti a penna e non ve n'e ignuno a stampa che se ne sarebe vergognato" (p. 398).

6. B.L. Ullmann, *The origins and development of humanistic script.* Rome 1960. J. Wardrop, *The Script of Humanism.* Oxford 1963. A.C. de la Mare, *The Handwriting of the Italian Humanists,* vol. I. Fascicule 1. Oxford 1973. O. Pächt, "Notes and observations on the origins of humanistic book decoration," *Fritz Saxl. A volume of memorial essays from his friends in England.* ed. D.J. Gordon. London 1957.

7. A.C. de la Mare, D.F.S. Thomson, "Poggio's earliest manuscript?" *Italia medioevale e umanistica* XVI (1973), 179–195. Color frontispiece to de la Mare, *Handwriting.*

8. O. Pächt, J.J.G. Alexander, *Illuminated manuscripts in the Bodleian Library, Oxford. 2. Italian school.* Oxford 1970, nos. 36, 210.

9. de la Mare, Thomson, p. 192.

10. Pächt, Alexander, no. 289.

11. J.J.G. Alexander, "A Virgil illuminated by Marco Zoppo," *Burlington Magazine.* CXI (1969), 514–17.

12. R. Chiarelli, *I codici miniati del Museo di San Marco a Firenze.* Florence 1968. M. Salmi, *La miniatura fiorentina gotica.* Florence 1954, pp. 45–46, tav. LII.

13. P. Toesca, *La pittura e la miniatura nella Lombardia.* 1912, reprinted Turin 1966.

14. A Stones, "An Italian miniature in the Gambier Parry collection," *Burlington Magazine* CXI (1969), 7–12. I. Toesca, "In margine al 'Maestro della Vitae Imperatorum'," *Paragone* XX (1969), 73–77. M. Levi d'Ancona, *The Wildenstein collection of Illuminations. The Lombard school.* Florence 1970, pp. 11 ff.

15. C. Huter, "Panel paintings by illuminators," *Arte Veneta* XXVIII (1974), 12–13.

16. J.J.G. Alexander, "The illuminated manuscripts of the 'Notitia Dignitatum'," *Aspects of the 'Notitia Dignitatum',* ed. R. Goodburn and P.

Bartholomew (*British Archeological Reports. Supplementary Series 15*). Oxford 1976.

17. B. Ashmole, "Cyriac of Ancona," *Proceedings of the British Academy.* XLV (1959), 25–41. For an account of the Renaissance attitude to classical antiquities see C.H. Mitchell, "Archaeology and Romance in Renaissance Italy," *Italian Renaissance Studies,* ed. E.F. Jacob. London 1960, pp. 455 ff.

18. C.H. Mitchell, "Felice Feliciano Antiquarius," *Proceedings of the British Academy* XLVII (1961), 197–221.

19. Pächt, Alexander, nos. 605, 606, pl. LVII.

20. C.H. Mitchell, *A fifteenth-century Italian Plutarch.* London 1961, p. 5. For the architectural frontispiece see M. Corbett, "The architectural title-page," *Motif* XII (1964), 49–62.

21. G. Mariani Canova, *La Miniatura Veneta del Rinascimento.* Venice 1969.

22. Wardrop, pls. 22, 23.

23. Mariani Canova, pp. 22, 24, 103–04. J.J.G. Alexander, "Notes on some Veneto-Paduan illuminated books of the Renaissance," *Arte Veneta* XXIII (1969), 9–10.

24. Belbello had himself been earlier in the position of completing another artist's work. See M. Meiss, E.W. Kirsch, *The Visconti Hours.* London 1972.

25. M.G. Ciardi Dupré, *I corali del Duomo di Siena.* Siena 1972.

26. T. de Marinis, *La Biblioteca Napoletana dei re d'Aragona,* 4 vols. Milan 1952, 1947. *Supplement,* 2 vols. Verona 1969.

27. J.J.G. Alexander, A.C. de la Mare, *The Italian manuscripts in the library of Major J.R. Abbey.* London 1969, pp. xxiii, xxviii, 37, 80.

28. Alexander, 'Notes,' p. 18.

29. P. D'Ancona, *La miniatura fiorentina,* I. p. 92, tav. xciii, II, pp. 772–84. Florence 1914.

30. Mariani Canova, pp. 26, 28, 30, 104–106. J.J.G. Alexander, "A manuscript of Petrarch's Rime and Trionfi," *Victoria and Albert Museum Yearbook* II (1970), 27–40.

31. E. Rodakiewicz, "The *editio princeps* of Roberto Valturio's 'De re militari' in relation to the Dresden and Munich manuscripts," *Maso Finiguerra* V (1940).

32. I. Malke, *Die Ausbreitung des verschollenen Urbildzyklus der Petrarca trionfi durch Cassoni in Florenz.* Berlin 1972.

33. A. Hobson, *Great Libraries.* London 1970, pp. 65–75.

# General Bibliography

P. D'Ancona, *La miniature italienne du X<sup>e</sup> au XVI<sup>e</sup> siècle*. Paris 1925.

S. S. Ludovici, *La miniatura rinascimentale*. Milan 1966.

*Mostra storica della miniatura*. Palazzo di Venezia. Rome 1954. Catalogo dal G. Muzzioli. Florence 1954.

M. Salmi, *Italian miniatures*. London 1957.

P. D'Ancona, E. Aeschlimann, *Dictionnaire des miniaturistes du Moyen Age et de la Renaissance dans les différentes contrées de l'Europe*. Milan 1949. Kraus reprint 1969.

# *Bibliography to Individual Manuscripts*

PLATES 1–2

D'Ancona, *Miniature italienne,* p. 78, pl. LXXV.

T. de Marinis, F. Rossi, "Notice sur les miniatures du 'Virgilius' de la Bibliothèque Riccardi de Florence," *Bulletin de la Société française de reproductions de manuscrits à peintures* XIII (1929), 17–31, pls. I-XII.

*Mostra storica,* no. 481, tav. LXIV, LXV b.

E. H. Gombrich, "Apollonio di Giovanni. A Florentine Cassone workshop seen through the eyes of a humanist poet," *Journal of the Warburg and Courtauld Institutes* XVIII (1955), 16–34.

B. Degenhart, A. Schmitt, *Corpus der Italienischen Zeichnungen 1300–1450.* Berlin 1968, pp. 559 ff. (Kat. 558), Abb. 798–803, Taf. 376–80.

B. Maracchi Biagiarelli, *Virgilius Opera.* Florence 1969 (complete facsimile).

E. Callmann, *Apollonio di Giovanni.* Oxford 1974, passim and plates.

PLATE 3

*Palaeographical Society,* II. London 1884, pl. 19.

G. Biagi, *Cinquanta tavole in fototipie da codici della R. Biblioteca Medicea Laurenziana.* Florence 1914, p. 12, tav. XXIV–XXVIII.

P. D'Ancona, *La Miniatura fiorentina.* Florence 1914, I, pp. 61–62, II, pp. 397–99.

*Mostra storica,* no. 499 (with misprint of date as 1458).

Salmi, *Italian miniatures,* p. 50, pl. XLIII b.

B. L. Ullmann, *The Origin and Development of Humanistic Script.* Rome 1960, p. 120.

M. Levi D'Ancona, *Miniatura e miniatori a Firenze dal XIV al XVI secolo.* Florence 1962, p. 110.

*La miniature italienne du X<sup>e</sup> au XVI<sup>e</sup> siècle.* Bruxelles, Bibliothèque Albert I<sup>e</sup>, Brussels 1969, no. 54 (date as 1458).

PLATES 4–5

Biagi, *cit.* (pl. 3), tav. XLVI–XLVII.

D'Ancona, *Miniatura Fiorentina, cit.* (pl. 3), I, pp. 49–50, 79 ff., tav. LXXXI–LXXXII, II, pp. 663–65.

A. de Hevesey, *La bibliothèque du roi Matthias Corvin.* Paris 1923, pp. 29–31, 65, pls. XXIII–IV.

*Mostra Storica,* no. 513.

C. Csapodi, K. Csapodi-Gárdonyi, *Biblioteca Corviniana.* Shannon 1969, p. 52, pls. XIII–XIV.

For Monte and Gherardo see M. Levi D'Ancona, *cit.* (pl. 3), pp. 127 ff., 199 ff. and E. Borsook, "Documenti relativi alle capelle di Lecceto e delle Selve di Filippo Strozzi," *Antichita Viva* III (1970).

PLATES 6–7

*A descriptive catalogue of fourteen illuminated manuscripts in the library of Henry Yates Thompson.* Cambridge 1914, pp. 66 ff., 123 ff.

*Illustrations from one hundred manuscripts in the library of Henry Yates Thompson,* VIII. London 1918, pp. 19–24, pls. LXX–LXXIX.

D'Ancona, *Miniature italienne,* p. 85.

J. Pope-Hennessy, *A Sienese Codex of the Divine Comedy.* Oxford, London 1947.

T. de Marinis, *La Biblioteca napoletana dei re d'Aragona.* Milan 1947, 1952, I, pp. 41, 74, II, pp. 62–63, III, tav. 81–87.

M. Meiss, "The Yates Thompson Dante and Priamo della Quercia," *Burlington Magazine* CVI (1964), 403–12.

*Reproductions from illuminated manuscripts. Series V,* British Museum 1965, p. 21, pl. XXXVIII.

P. Brieger, M. Meiss, C. Singleton, *Illustrated manuscripts of the Divine Comedy.* New York, London 1970, pp. 70–80, 269–75, pls. *passim.*

PLATES 8–10

H. Martin, "Sur un portrait de Jacques-Antoine Marcello," *Mémoires et Bulletin de la Société Nationale des Antiquaires de France* 6ᵉ ser. IX (1900), 229–67.

H. Martin, P. Lauer, *Les principaux manuscrits à peintures de la bibliothèque de l'Arsenal.* Paris 1929, pls. 51–52.

M. Meiss, *Andrea Mantegna as illuminator.* Hamburg 1957.

G. Robertson, *Giovanni Bellini.* Oxford 1968, pp. 17–21, 28, pls. II b, III, IV a.

G. Mariani Canova, *La Miniatura Veneta del Rinascimento.* Venice 1969, pp. 16, 141, tav. 1, figs. 1–3.

PLATES 11–12

G. Milanesi, *Storia della miniatura italiana con documenti inediti* in G. Vasari, *Le Vite,* VII. Florence 1850, pp. 282 ff.

M. Salmi, "Gerolamo da Cremona, miniatore e pittore," *Bolletino d'Arte* ser. 2, II (1922), 396, figs. 15–18.

D'Ancona, *Miniature italienne,* p. 60.

L. Thorndike, *A History of Magic and Experimental Science,* IV. New York 1934, p. 620 and ch. XXXVIII.

*Mostra storica,* no. 619.

M. Levi D'Ancona, "Postille a Girolamo da Cremona," *Studi di Bibliografia e di Storia in onore di Tammaro de Marinis,* III. Verona 1964, pp. 45–104.

Canova, *Miniatura Veneta, cit.* (pls. 8–10), pp. 60, 119, fig. 86.

PLATES 13–14

The present manuscript is unpublished and I owe knowledge of it to M. François Avril, Bibliothèque Nationale. For Bartolomeo Sanvito see J. Wardrop, *The Script of Humanism.* Oxford 1963. J. Ruysschaert, *Archivio della Società Romana di storia patria* XX (1967), 367. J. J. G. Alexander, A. C. de la Mare, *The Italian manuscripts in the library of Major J. R. Abbey.* London 1969, pp. 105–10. For the faceted or prismatic capitals see Meiss, *cit.* (pls. 8–10). For the Turin *Historia Augusta* see B. Degenhart, "Ludovico II Gonzaga in einer Miniatur Pisanello's," *Pantheon* XXX (1972), especially p. 198 and notes 23–24.

PLATES 15–16

H. J. Hermann, *Beschreibendes Verzeichnis der illuminierten Handschriften in Oesterreich, VIII, Band 6, Teil 2. Oberitalien: Venetien.* Leipzig 1931, pp. 190–200, Taf. LVIII–LXIII.

E. Trenkler, "Les principaux manuscrits à peintures de la bibliothèque nationale de Vienne," *Bulletin de la Société française de reproductions de manuscrits à peintures* XX (1937), 36–37, pl. Vb.

Salmi, *Italian miniatures,* p. 67, fig. 85.

Canova, *Miniatura Veneta, cit.* (pls. 8–10), pp. 36, 108–09, tav. 11–13, fig. 55 a, b.

PLATES 17–18

H. Y. Thompson, "The most magnificent book in the world?" *Burlington*

*Magazine* IX (1906), 16–21.

B. Berenson, "Una nuova pittura di Girolamo da Cremona," *Rassegna d'Arte* VII (1907), 35.

M. Levi D'Ancona, "Postille," *cit.* (pls. 11–12), fig. XIII.

J. J. G. Alexander, "Notes on some Veneto-Paduan illuminated books of the Renaissance," *Arte Veneta* XXIII (1969), 10.

Canova, *Miniatura Veneta, cit.* (pls. 8–10), pp. 58, 62, 64, 120–21, 127–29, tav. 22–23, figs. 90, 94.

PLATES 19–22

H. J. Hermann, "Zur Geschichte der Miniaturmalerei am Hofe der Este in Ferrara," *Jahrbuch der Kunsthistorischen Sammlungen des Allerhöchsten Kaiserhauses,* XXI (1900), 114–271, Taf. XI–XVIII, Fig. 12–32.

D'Ancona, *Miniature italienne,* pp. 65–67, pls. LVIII–IX.

D. Fava, *I tesori delle Biblioteche Italiane: Emilia e Romagna.* Milan 1932, pp. 154, 173, 326, tav. 23, 30.

*La Bibbia di Borso d'Este,* complete facsimile, ed. A. Venturi, 2 vols. Milan 1937.

D. Fava, M. Salmi, *I manoscritti miniati della biblioteca Estense di Modena,* I. Florence 1950, pp. 90–133, tav. XX–XXVIII.

*Mostra storica,* no. 546, tav. LXX.

Salmi, *Italian miniatures,* pp. 58–59, pls. L–LIII.

M. Salmi, *Pittura e miniatura a Ferrara nel primo Rinascimento.* Milan 1961, pp. 22–30, tav. VI–VIII, 16–20.

M. Righetti, "Indagine su Gerolamo da Cremona," *Arte Lombarda* XLI (1974), 32–42, tav. 4–8.

PLATES 23–26

F. Hermannin, "Le miniature ferraresi della Biblioteca Vaticana," *L'Arte* III (1900), 341–73, figs. 2–9.

H. J. Hermann, *cit.* (pls. 19–22), pp. 178 ff.

*Miniatures of the Renaissance. Exhibition for the Fifth Centenary of the Vatican Library.* 1950, no. 42, pl. IV.

L. Michelini Tocci, M. Salmi, G. Petrocchi, *Il Dante Urbinate (Codice Urbinate Latino 365).* Vatican 1965, complete color facsimile and full description with earlier bibliography.

P. Brieger, M. Meiss, C. Singleton, *cit.* (pls. 6–7), pp. 44, 48, 90, 113, 331–32.

PLATES 27–28

H. J. Hermann, *cit.* (pls. 19–22), pp. 90 ff.

G. Bertoni, C. Bonacini, *De Sphaera.* Modena, 1914.

F. Malaguzzi Valeri, *La corte di Ludovico il Moro. Gli artisti Lombardi,* III. Milan 1917 (reprinted 1970), pp. 144–47.

F. Wittgens, "Cristorofo de Predis," *La Bibliofilia* XXXVI (1934), 368–70.

*Mostra storica,* no. 653.

S. Samek Ludovici, *Il 'De Sphaera' Estense e l'iconografia astrologica.* Milan 1958 (reproducing all miniatures).

*Arte Lombarda dai Visconti agli Sforza.* Palazzo reale, Milan 1958, no. 347.

P. Puliatti, *Il 'De Sphaera' Estense.* Bergamo 1969.

*La miniature italienne du X<sup>e</sup> au XVI<sup>e</sup> siècle,* Bruxelles, Bibliothèque Albert I<sup>e</sup>. Brussels 1969, no. 86, pl. 31.

D. Fava, M. Salmi, *I manoscritti miniati della Biblioteca Estense di Modena,* II. Florence 1973, pp. 25–27, tav. XI.

PLATES 29–32

D'Ancona, *Miniature italienne,* p. 56, pl. LIII.

Malaguzzi Valeri, *cit.* (pls. 27–28), I, Milan 1929 (reprinted 1970), pp. 413 ff, tav. IV, XV, XVIII, XX, XXIV, III, Milan 1917, pp. 162 ff. IV, Milan 1923, pp. 28–29, tav. VII.

D. Fava, "Documenti artistici della educazione dei principi nella corte sforzesca di Milano," *Accademie e*

*Biblioteche d'Italia* XX (1952), 24–30.

*Mostra storica,* no. 661.

Salmi, *Italian miniatures,* pp. 72–74, pl. XXI a.

E. Pellegrin, *La bibliothèque des Visconti et des Sforza, ducs de Milan, au XVe siècle.* Paris 1955, espec. pp. 382–83.

B. Horodyski Bogdan, "Birago miniaturiste des Sforza," *Scriptorium* X (1956), 251–55.

*Arte Lombarda, cit.* (pls. 27–28), no. 454, tav. CLXXIX.

C. Santoro, *I codici miniati della biblioteca Trivulziana.* Milan 1958, pp. 40–42, tav. XXIX–XXXIV.

De Marinis, *cit. Legatura* (pls. 38–39), III, no. 2598, tav. CCCCXXXIII.

C. Santoro, *I codici medioevali della Biblioteca Trivulziana.* Milan 1965, pp. 318–19.

G. Bologna, *Miniature Lombarde della Biblioteca Trivulziana.* Milan 1973, pp. 44–45.

PLATES 33–34

R. Beer, "Les principaux manuscrits à peintures de la bibliothèque imperiale de Vienne," *Bulletin de la Société française de reproductions de manuscrits à peintures,* III (1913), 35, 48, pl. XL.

E. Trenkler, *ibid.,* XX (1937), 64–66.

D'Ancona, *Miniature italienne,* p. 91, tav. XC.

H. J. Hermann, *Beschreibendes Verzeichnis der illuminierten Handschriften in Oesterreich, VIII. Band 6, Teil 4. Unteritalien.* Leipzig 1933, pp. 50–57, Taf. XVIII–XXI.

T. de Marinis, *cit.* (pls. 6–7), I, pp. 8, 50, 74 n. 29, II, pp. 47–48, III, tav. 61–66.

PLATES 35–37

H. J. Hermann, "Miniaturhandschriften aus der Bibliothek des Herzogs Andrea Matteo III Acquaviva," *Jahrbuch der Kunsthistorischen Sammlungen des Allerhöchsten Kaiserhauses*

XIX (1898), 147–216, Taf. VI–XII, figs. 5–7.

D'Ancona, *Miniature italienne,* p. 92, pl. XCI.

H. J. Hermann, *Beschreibendes Verzeichnis der illuminierten Handschriften in Oesterreich, VIII. Band VI, Teil 4. Unteritalien.* Leipzig 1933, pp. 79–105, Taf. XXXIV–XLIII.

E. Trenkler, "Les principaux manuscrits à peintures de la bibliothèque nationale de Vienne," *Bulletin de la Société française de reproductions de manuscrits à peintures* XX (1937), 36–38, pl. XLII.

F. Unterkircher, *European illuminated manuscripts in the Austrian National Library.* London 1967, pp. 156 ff., pl. 36.

PLATES 38–39

*Palaeographical Society,* II. London 1885, pl. 38.

*A descriptive catalogue of twenty illuminated manuscripts, Nos. LXXV–XCIV, in the collection of Henry Yates Thompson.* Cambridge 1907, pp. 145–52 (entry by S. C. Cockerell).

*Illustrations from one hundred manuscripts in the library of Henry Yates Thompson,* VI. London 1916, pp. 36–42, pls. 79–88.

D'Ancona, *Miniature italienne,* pp. 73, 88, pls. LXVIII, LXXXV.

J. Wardrop, "Pierantonio Sallando and Girolamo Pagliorolo, scribes to Giovanni II Bentivoglio," *Signature* n.s. II (1946), 4–30, fig. 14.

P. P. Bober, *Drawings after the Antique by Amico Aspertini. Sketchbooks in the British Museum.* London 1957, p. 136, fig. 135.

Salmi, *Italian miniatures,* pp. 57, 64, figs. 72, 80.

T. de Marinis, *La legatura artistica in Italia nei secoli XV e XVI,* II. Florence 1960, pp. 57, 81 (no. 1658), tav. CCC, CCCI.

*Reproductions from illuminated manu-*

scripts, Series V. British Museum 1965, pls. XLV–XLVI.

N. Dacos, *La découverte de la Domus Aurea et la formation des grotesques à la Renaissance.* London 1969, p. 82.

PLATE 40

P. D'Ancona, "Di alcuni codici miniati conservati nelle biblioteche tedesche e austriache," *L'Arte* X (1907), 28–30.

D'Ancona, *Miniature italienne,* p. 63, pl. LVI.

W. Hopf, *Die Landesbibliothek Kassel 1580–1930.* Marburg 1930, pp. 105–08, Taf. 16.

M. Levi D'Ancona, "Un libro d'ore di Francesco Marmitta da Parma e Martino da Modena al Museo Correr–II°," *Bolletino dei Musei Civici Veneziani* XII (1967), 9–28, fig. 4.

# List of Color Plates

# List of Black-and-White Figures

# PLATES
# AND
# COMMENTARIES

PLATE 1

VIRGIL, WORKS
fol. 18 *Georgics, I*

This manuscript contains the three main works of the Roman poet Virgil (d. 19 B.C.): the *Eclogues,* the *Georgics,* and the *Aeneid.* The illumination was never completed. Eighty-eight miniatures were executed, eighty-six being illustrations to the *Aeneid* (ff. 61v–104v), the remaining two being the frontispieces to the *Eclogues* and *Georgics.* The last eight miniatures in the Aeneid (ff. 101–104v) are drawings, and twelve other miniatures are only partly painted and gilded (ff. 93–98v).

Virgil is one of the very few classical authors of whose works we have illustrated copies from the Late Antique period. Two manuscripts, both incomplete, survive, the so-called *Virgilius Vaticanus* of c. 400 A.D. and the *Virgilius Romanus* of probably the fifth century. Though Virgil was read throughout the Middle Ages it seems that there was no continuous tradition of illustration, and that the Renaissance illuminators had to create their own cycles of illustrations afresh. All the pictures here are in the lower margins, and since they generally relate closely to the lines of text written immediately above them, and since no other surviving Virgil is illuminated on such a scale, they are likely to be in most, if not all, cases the invention of the artist. The scene shown here illustrates the first book of the *Georgics,* which concerns the growing of arable crops, so we see ploughing, harrowing, digging and sowing. In the background, to the left, by a total anachronism the artist has represented some cowled religious.

The illumination is attributed to the Florentine artist Apollonio di Giovanni who died in 1465. He was mainly active as a painter of marriage chests (*cassoni*). The date of the manuscript is probably c. 1450–60.

## PRAEFATIO LIBRORVM GEORGICO-
## RVM INCIPIT FOELICITER

Vid faciat letaf segetef, quo sidere seruet
Agricola, ut facilem terram pscindat aratrif.
Semina que tacienda, modof cultufq locorum
Et docuit, messef magno olim fenore reddi.

## LIBER PRIMVS GEORGICORVM IN
## CIPIT FOELICITER.

Vid faciat letaf segetef, quo
sidere terram
Vertere mecennaf, ulimifq
adiungere uitef
Conueniat, que cura boum
quif cultuf habendo
Sit pecori, apibuf quanta
experientia parcif.
hinc canere incipiam. Vof o
clariffima mundi

l. umina Libentem celo que ducitif annum
l. iber et alma ceref, uestro hunc munere tellus
c. alconiam pingui glandem mutauit arista.
p. oculaq inuentif acheloia miscuit uuif
e. t uof agrestum presentia numina telluf faum
F. erte simul faunıq, pedem ...dryadefq puellg
M. unere uestra cano, tuq, o cui prima frementem

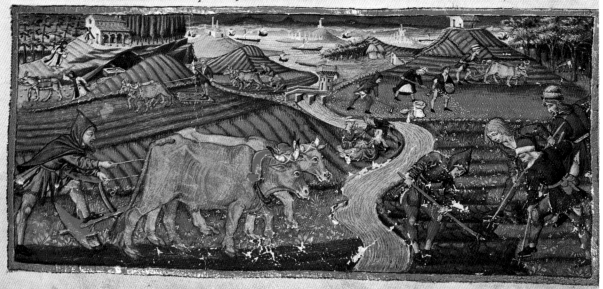

Q uarum que forma pulcherrima deiopeam
C onnubio iungam stabili · propriamq, dicabo ·
O mnes ut tecum meritis pro talibus annos
E xigat · et pulchra faciat te prole parentem
E olus hec contra · tuus o regina quid optes
E xplorare labor · mihi iussa capessere fas est ·
T u mihi quodcunq, hoc regni · tu sceptra iouemq,
C oncilias · tu das epulis occumbere diuum ·
N imborumq, facis tempestatumq, potentem
h ec ubi dicta cauum conuersa cuspide montem
I mpulit in latus · ac uenti uelut agmine facto
Q ua data porta ruunt · et terras turbine perflant
I ncubuere mari · totumq, a sedibus imis
V na eurusq, notusq, ruunt · creberq, procellis
A fricus et uastos uoluunt ad litora fluctus ·
I nsequitur clamorq, uirum · stridorq, rudentum
E ripiunt subito nubes celumq, diemq,
T eucrorum ex oculis · ponto nox incubat atra
I ntonuere poli · et crebris micat ignibus ether ·
P resentemq, uiris intentant omnia mortem ·
E x templo enee soluuntur frigore membra ·
I ngemit · et duplices tendens ad sidera palmas
T alia uoce refert · oterq, quaterq, beati ·
Q uis ante ora patrum troie sub mensibus altis
C ontigit oppetere · o danaum fortissime gentis
T itide me ne iliacis occumbere campis

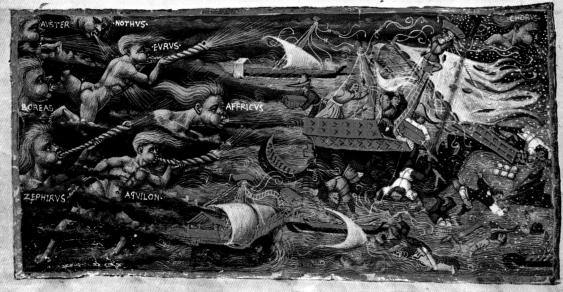

## PLATE 2

Virgil, Works
fol. 62v *Aeneid, I*

In this miniature the storm is represented in which Aeneas' fleet is wrecked and driven onto the coast of Africa near Carthage (Aeneid, I, lines 72–101 are written above). On the left we see the Winds shown as naked classical personifications blowing horns and blasting the ships whose masts break as the crews are thrown into the water. The same scene is shown very similarly in one of a pair of *cassone* panels from Apollonio's shop now in the Yale University Art Gallery.

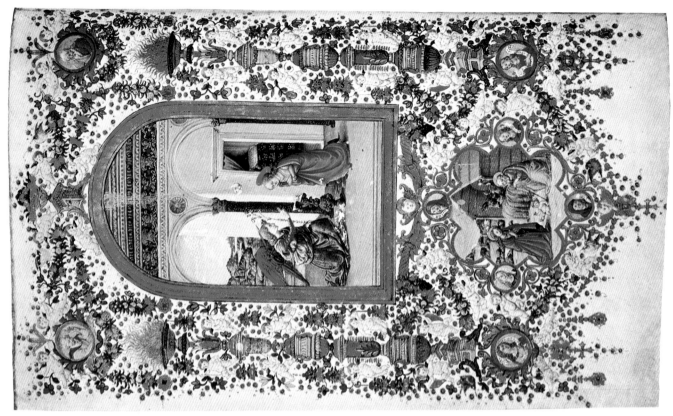

3a

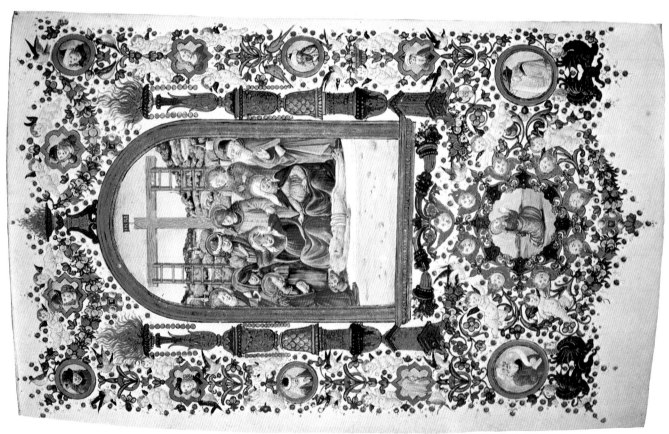

3b

## PLATE 3

THE HOURS OF LORENZO DEI MEDICI
a) fol. 13v *The Annunciation*
b) fol. 228v *The Lamentation*

This little Book of Hours (that is a devotional book with prayers to be said at various hours of the day) was written in humanistic script by Antonio Sinnibaldi who signed and dated it 1485. Born in 1443, he was one of the leading calligraphers in Florence in the late fifteenth century. In a tax declaration of 1480, although no doubt exaggerating in order to reduce his liability, he said his work had been so reduced by the invention of printing that it hardly kept him in clothes.

Since the borders contain the Medici emblems, it has been conjectured that the manuscript was made for Lorenzo dei Medici (1448–92). Poet and man of letters, as well as patron of the arts, Lorenzo escaped the Pazzi conspiracy of 1478, in which his brother, Giuliano, was killed, and continued to virtually rule the city until his death, although it remained in name a republic. By the seventeenth century the manuscript was in the Netherlands, where entries were made of the births of the sons of Maximilian, Count of Merode. Later it was acquired by the 4th Earl of Ashburnham from the notorious book thief, Guglielmo Libri. The Italian Government bought Lord Ashburnham's most important Italian manuscripts in 1884.

Folio 13v (a) shows the Annunciation, commonly used to introduce Prime, the first hour of the day. Below, the Nativity is shown in the ornate border which also contains the three feathers, one of the Medici emblems.

Folio 228v (b), preceding the little Hours of the Cross, shows the Lamentation with Christ laid on the ground, an unusual iconography suggesting Netherlandish influence. Like the other miniatures, this is in a frame with a rounded top and a molding below like the frame of an altarpiece, an effect enhanced by the lighted candelabra. The owner is presented, therefore, with a little private chapel for his own use.

## PLATE 4

BIBLE OF MATTHIAS CORVINUS
fol. 1v *King David in Prayer*

This is the third volume of a Bible made in Florence for Matthias Corvinus, King of Hungary. He had been elected to the throne in 1458 when he was seventeen, and proved an able administrator as well as a successful soldier. The influence of Italian humanistic culture was already strong in Hungary, and Matthias continued to encourage humanist scholars at the Court and to cultivate close relations with Italy. In 1476 he married, as his second wife, Beatrice of Aragon, daughter of King Ferrante of Naples. He founded the University of Buda, patronized Italian architects and artists, and built up the great library which formed, at the time, the largest single collection of Italian manuscripts outside Italy. In 1461 the Italian humanist Marzio Galeotto was appointed *praefectus bibliotecae Budensis,* and he was succeeded by the Florentine Taddeo Ugoletto.

The frontispiece to the Psalms shows King David in prayer with his victory over Goliath seen in the distance. To the left, the young shepherd boy picks a pebble from the stream for his sling. To the right, before the walls of Jerusalem, the Israelites bearing a banner with the arms of the Christian kingdom of Jerusalem pursue the fleeing Philistines, who are represented as Turks with turbans. In the center, David cuts off the giant's head.

Matthias was constantly engaged in war with the Turks on his southeastern borders, and the political situation seems to be further referred to in the miniature, since in the middle distance three figures (the foremost of whom is Matthias himself) watch the battle. The second figure, on the right, is King Charles VIII of France with his crown and scepter, (in 1487 Matthias' envoys were seeking an alliance with Charles VIII), and the third is presumably another French prince, since his robe is covered with fleur-de-lys. Various conjectures have been made as to the identity of this third figure, none generally accepted.

# PLATE 5

BIBLE OF MATTHIAS CORVINUS
fol. 2 *Opening of the Psalter*

On the facing page the text begins with Psalm I and part of Psalm II written in gold on purple. David in armor, but with helmet and sword laid aside, is seated playing the Psaltery. The Holy Spirit hovers overhead to inspire him. In the miniature, above, Hebron, where David was crowned, is represented as the city of Florence with the Palazzo Vecchio, the Loggia dei Lanzi and the Cathedral all visible. In the foreground the Israelites, led by David, fight the Philistines. The bust figures in roundels in the borders are, on the left, Melchisedech and David's musicians, Aseph and Idythun, and, on the right, Solomon, Moses, and Abraham. A roundel is left blank in the border below for Matthias' arms, but to the left the arms of Hungary, Dalmatia and Galicia have been inserted.

In the 1480s Matthias was employing scribes in Florence to copy manuscripts, and Ugoletto was sent there to buy more manuscripts. However, when Matthias died in 1490 many manuscripts had not yet been sent off to him, and others, such as the present Bible, were not yet finished. His successor, Ladislaus, wrote to the Signoria in 1498 to try to recover them. The reply was that a number were now in the hands of the Medici (who had been Matthias' bankers) and this Bible, which was valued at the huge sum of 1400 gold ducats, was among them. Perhaps it was lucky that the Bible never left Florence, for in 1526 the Turks sacked Buda and much of Matthias' great library was destroyed or dispersed.

The illumination has been attributed to the brothers Gherardo and Monte di Giovanni di Miniato; the former was born in 1446 and died in 1497, while the latter was born in 1448 and died c. 1532–33. A number of documented works exist for each of the brothers, but the task of separating their hands has yet to be undertaken in detail.

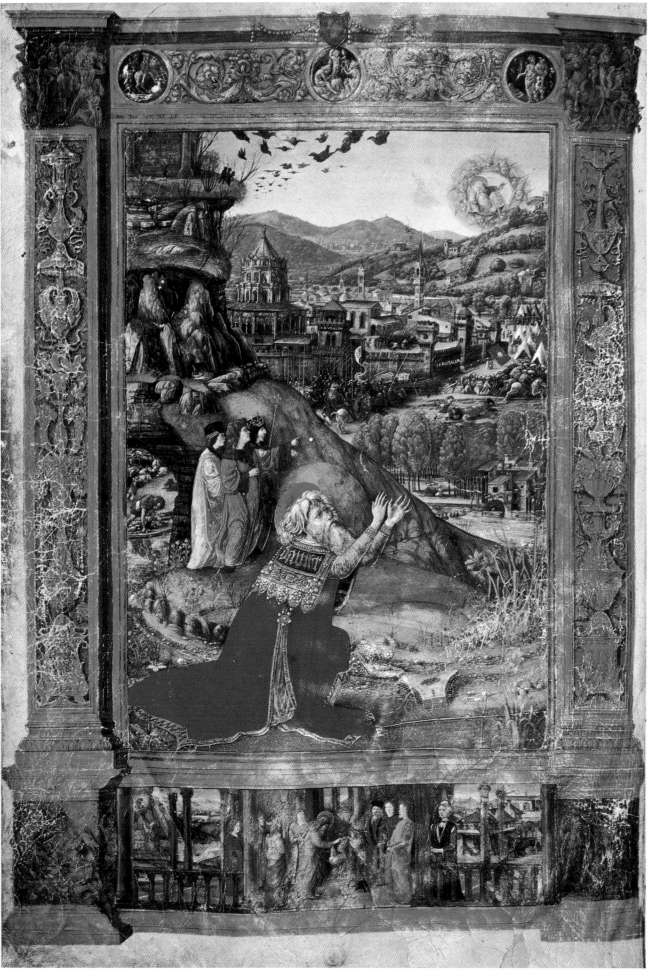

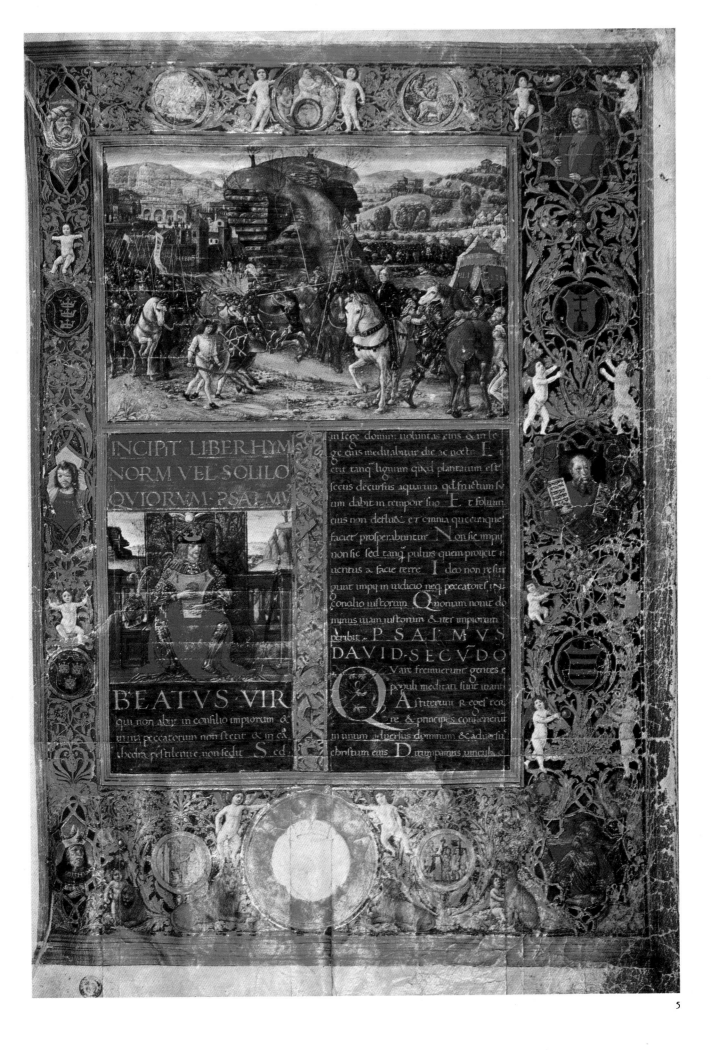

## PLATE 6

DANTE, LA DIVINA COMMEDIA
fol. 20 *Inferno, Canto XI*

Illustrations for Dante's great poem of his visionary journey through Hell and Purgatory to Paradise were created soon after it was written. Some of the early fourteenth-century manuscripts already use a system of historiated initials introducing the three books and a series of illustrations running along the lower margin and thus closely integrated with the text of the various cantos. The same arrangement is followed in the present manuscript, which was made for Alfonso of Aragon, King of Aragon, Naples and Sicily (1416–58), in Siena (bearing his arms on folio 1). There are altogether one hundred and twelve framed miniatures and three historiated initials.

Two artists worked on the manuscript, of whom the first, seen here, has been identified by Millard Meiss as Priamo della Quercia on the basis of comparisons with a documented fresco in the Spedale in Siena of 1442. Meiss drew attention to the luminous color of these miniatures and suggested the influence of Domenico Veneziano, proposing a date on stylistic grounds of c. 1442–50 for the miniatures.

The scene here is from *Inferno,* Canto XI. Virgil and Dante stand on the left behind the tomb of the heretic Pope Anastasius. They are on the rim of the sixth circle of Hell and pause to accustom themselves to the stench rising from below. Virgil explains the structure of Hell and that the three rings of the sixth circle contain those violent against the laws of God, against themselves, and against others. The miniature is original in showing the scene in this way with the bands of contorted naked bodies. The interest in studies of the nude from life is typical of the Renaissance.

Et io maestro assai chiara procede
la tua ragion et assai ben distingue
questo baratro el popol chel possede

A dime quei della palude pigre
che menal uento et che bacte lapiogia
et chessincontra consi aspre lingue

Per che no dentro della cita rogia
sonei puniti se dio glia in ira
et se noglia pche sonadtal fogia

Et egli adme pche tanto delira
disse longengnio tuo daquel che sole
ouer lamente douialtroue mira

Non tirimenbra diquelle parole
conle quai la tua ethica ptracta
le tre dispofition che idio no uole

Incontinenza malitie la macta
bestialtade et como incontinenza
mendio offende et men biasino accacta

Se tu riguardi ben questa sentenza
et rechitalamente chi son quelli
che su difuor sostengon penitenza

Tu uederai ben pche questi felli
sian dipirtati et pche men crocciata
la diuina uendecta li martelli

Sol che sani ogni uista turbata
tu mi contenti si qn tu solui
che no men che sauer dubiar magrata

Ancor un poco indietro ti riuolui
diffio la doue dichusura offende
la diuina bontade elgroppo solue

Fia mi disse auchi lantende
nota no pur in una sola pte
come natura lo suo corso prende

Dal diuin intellecto et da sua arte
et se tu ben la tua phisica noce
tu trouerai no do po molte carte

Che larte uostra quella quato pote
segue comel maestro sul discente
siche uostrarte adio quase nipote

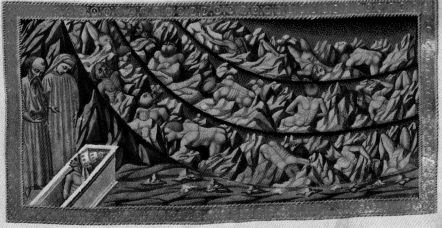

## PLATE 7

### DANTE, LA DIVINA COMMEDIA
### fol. 145 *Paradiso, Canto IX*

The second artist of the manuscript is the Sienese painter Giovanni di Paolo, who was active from 1426 until his death in 1482. All his miniatures are in *Paradiso.* The present one illustrates Canto IX. Dante, accompanied by Beatrice in the Heaven of Venus, meets Cunizza of Treviso and Folco of Marseilles, bishop of Toulouse. Folco prophesies retribution on Florence, the city of the Devil, which has corrupted Popes and Cardinals with its gold florins stamped with the fleur-de-lys. The interest of the miniature is in its depiction of the city of Florence with the Duomo in the center. This, with another representation of the Cathedral on folio 159, again provides evidence for a dating of the manuscript in the 1440s, since neither the three exedras of the Cathedral designed by Brunelleschi and completed in 1444, nor his lantern to the dome, on which work started in 1446, are represented.

The manuscript was later in the convent library of San Miguel, Valencia, in Spain, founded by Ferdinand, Duke of Calabria, in 1538. It was acquired in 1901 by the great collector of fine illuminated manuscripts, Henry Yates Thompson, and bequeathed to the British Museum by Mrs. Yates Thompson in 1941 (Plates 17–18, 38–39).

Piangera feltro ancora la difalta
dellinpio suo pastor che fara sconcia
siche psimul nõ fintro imalta

Troppo farrebe larga la bigontia
che receuessel sangue ferrarese
et stanco chil pefasse a oncia a oncia

Che donera questo pre cortese
pmostrarse de parte et cotai doni
conformi fieno al uiuer del paese

Vsonospechi et uoi dicete troui
onde rifolge ānoi dio giudicante
siche questi parlarmi puon boni

Qui si tacecte et fecemi senbiante
che fosse ad altro uolta pla rota
in che se mise comera dauante

Laltra leticia chemera gia nota
pclara cosa mise fece iuista
qual fin balascio iche il sol pcota

Per leticiar lassu folgol sacquita
si come riso qui ma giu sabuia
lonbra defuor come la mēt e trista

Io uede tucto et tucto ueder fe inluya
diffio beato spirto si che nulla
uoglia dite adfe potessei fuya

Vnqz lauoce tua chel ciel trastulla
senp col canto di que fochi py
che de sei ali facian la cuculla

Per che nõ foclisfice ai miei desiri
gia nõ actenderei0 tua dimanda
fe mintuiasse come tucti imy

La magior ualle in che lacqua sispanda
in cominciaro allor le sue parole
fuor diquella mar che la terra igherlanda

Tra discordanti liti contral sole
tanto senua che fa meridiano
la doue lorizonte pfa far sole

Diquella ualle fuio litorano
tra ebro et magra che pcamin corto
parte lo genouese dal toscano

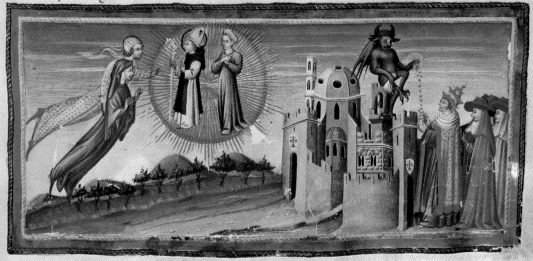

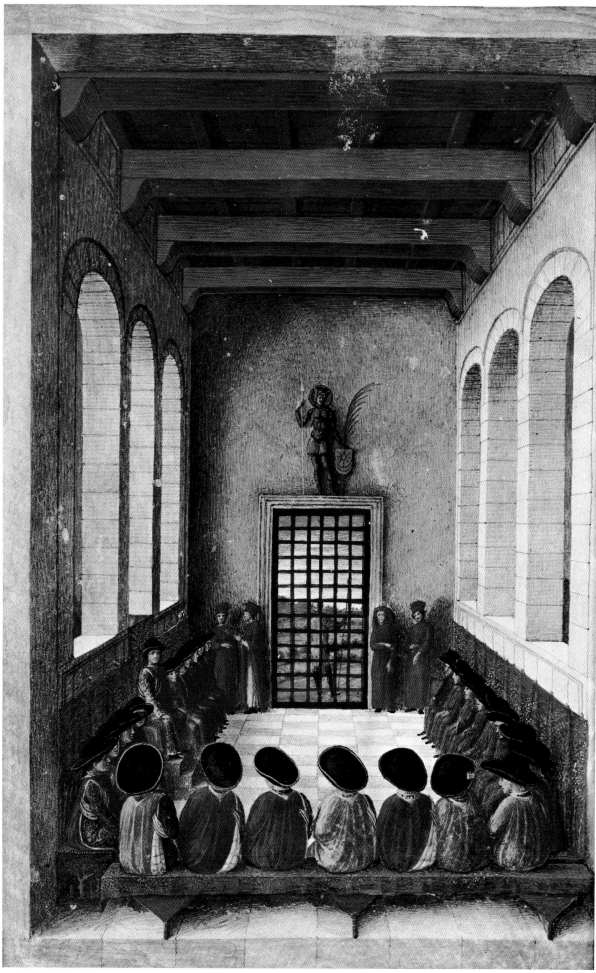

## PLATE 8

### LIFE AND PASSION OF SAINT MAURICE
fol. Cv *Congress of Knights of the Crescent*

This precious little manuscript was sent as a present from the Venetian general, Jacopo Marcello, to Jean Cossa, seneschal of Provence and councillor of René of Anjou, on June 1, 1453. René was on the point of invading Italy in the hope of recovering the Kingdom of Naples from the Aragonese. He counted on the support of Francesco Sforza, who had become Duke of Milan in 1450, and of Florence. Sforza, however, was then at war with Venice and hoping for help from the French, and it seems that Marcello was trying to influence Cossa, and through him René, with a timely present.

Three years before, at an earlier stage in the complicated maneuvers over Sforza's succession and René's claims, Marcello had expressed support for René, and had been rewarded by membership in René's newly founded chivalric Order of the Crescent. He was elected a knight on August 26, 1449 and admitted in 1450, when Cossa presided as annual senator.

The present miniature represents the Order in conclave, with twenty-five knights seated on benches in a hall. They wear the scarlet cloaks and black hats rimmed in gold prescribed in the statutes, and each has a gold crescent under his arm. On the far wall is a statue of the patron saint of the Order, Saint Maurice.

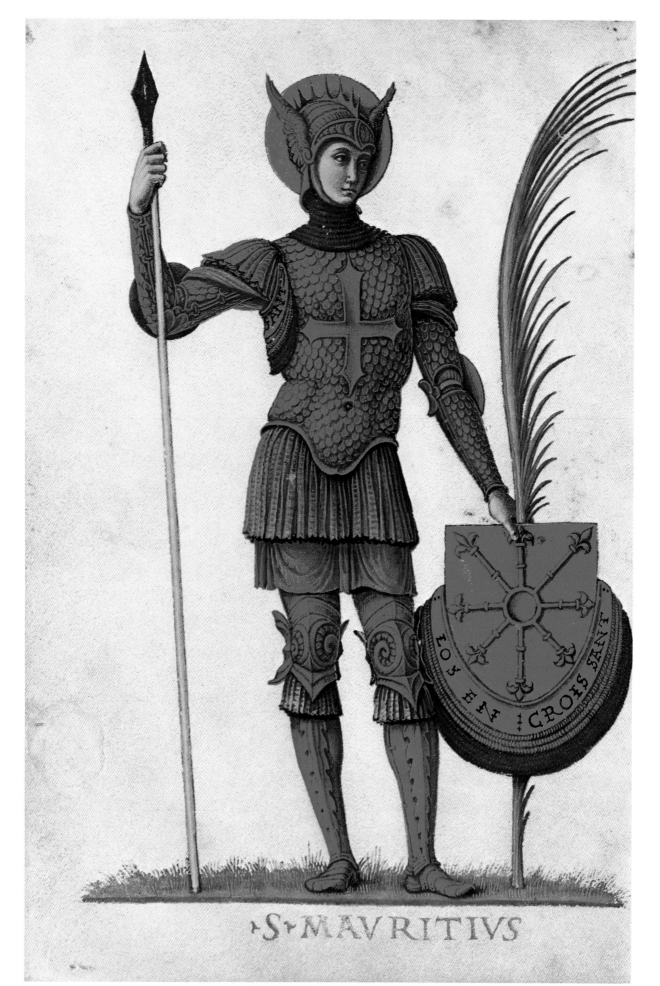

·S·MAVRITIVS

PLATE 9

LIFE AND PASSION OF SAINT MAURICE
fol. 34v *Saint Maurice*

The Life of the patron of the Order, Saint Maurice, contains seven small miniatures by a Lombard illuminator. It is followed by a poem in hexameters in praise of the saint by Marcello himself, added by a different scribe. The present miniature prefaces the poem. Saint Maurice was a member of the Theban legion, so-called because its members were recruited in upper Egypt. He was believed to have been martyred with his fellow Christians in Gaul under Maximian, c. 287 A.D. He is represented here holding in his left hand the palm of martyrdom and a shield showing his arms, with the crescent and the motto of the Order, *Los en croisant*, below. His armor is not contemporary and is intended to look antique.

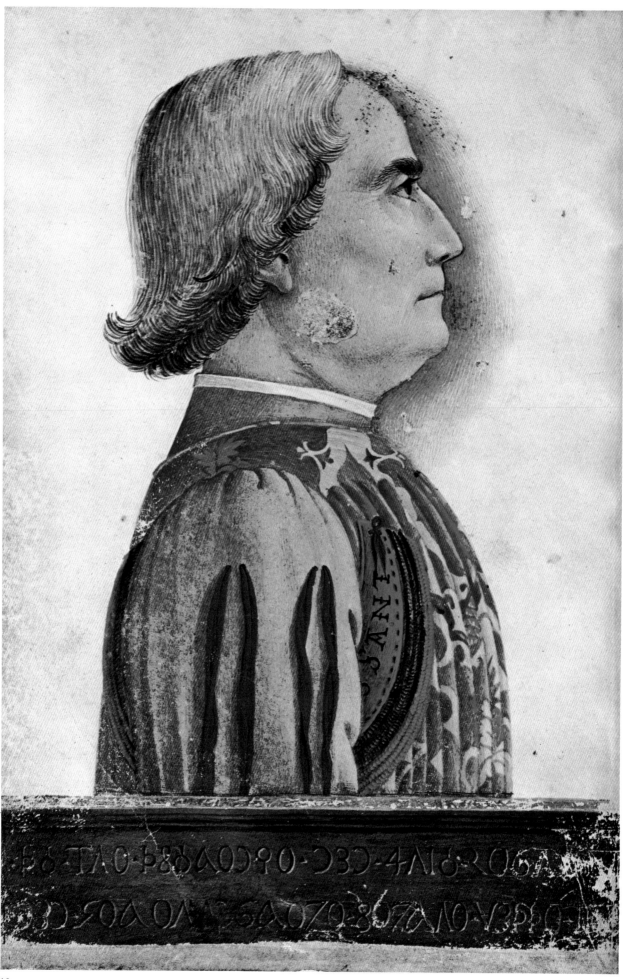

10

## PLATE 10

LIFE AND PASSION OF SAINT MAURICE
fol. 38v *Jacopo Marcello*

At the end of the manuscript are a pair of miniatures facing each other. The one on the verso is a portrait of Marcello, once again dressed as a member of the Order. On the parapet is a message in code first deciphered by Henri Martin, Conservateur of the Arsenal library. It reads: *Se mia speranza non dixe bugia non farai ingrata patria Cossa mia*, which Meiss translates as: "If my hopes do not deceive me, you, Cossa, will not make my country ungrateful to you." This must refer to the political situation as outlined.

The quality of this splendid portrait led Meiss to attribute it to Andrea Mantegna (c. 1431–1506), who was the adopted son of the Paduan painter, Francesco Squarcione (1397–1468). He considers the miniature of the Chapter also to be by Mantegna and the other two pages to be his, but probably completed with assistance. In January 1448, Mantegna secured his independence from Squarcione, against whom, however, he later had a number of lawsuits, and in the same year he undertook part of the decoration of the Ovetari chapel in the church of the Eremitani, Padua, on which he was still at work in 1453. The figure of Saint Maurice here shows similarities to some of the Eremitani figures. In the next year, 1454, he married Nicolosia, daughter of Jacopo Bellini, and Meiss noted the influence of Jacopo in these miniatures. Other attributions have been made, for example to the illuminator Leonardo Bellini and to Girolamo da Cremona (Plates 11–12), but as Robertson rightly says: "Nobody who has taken the trouble to examine the manuscript could doubt that the miniatures are the work of a major artist." Robertson himself makes out a case for their being by Giovanni Bellini, Jacopo's son, who seems to have been born in the same year as Mantegna.

PLATE 11

PSEUDO-LULL, ALCHEMICAL TREATISES
fol. 114v *Alchemical Diagram*

The chimerical hope of transmuting base metals into the precious metals, silver
or gold, by alchemy continued to delude men of the Renaissance, and long
after, as is shown by Ben Johnson's *The Alchemist*. The body of texts in the
present manuscript are ascribed to the Spanish theologian and mystic, Raymund
Lull (c. 1235–c. 1315), in spite of the expressions of scepticism and disap-
proval of alchemy found in his genuine works. None of these pseudo-Lullian
texts is in fact likely to have been written before the middle or even the end
of the fourteenth century. Unfortunately there is no indication as to who was
the owner of this particularly splendid copy. The main text to which the diagrams here and on the next page refer, is the *Testamentum* of which Thorndike says: "it seems in many respects the keystone or backbone of the Lullian
alchemical collection." It consists of three parts, theoretical, practical, and
thirdly, the Book of Mercuries. It was believed that the precious metals could
be formed from special preparations of quicksilver and sulphur. Several
manuscripts claim that the *Testament* was composed by Lull in London where
he had gone to manufacture gold for King Edward in the Tower!

# PLATE 12

PSEUDO-LULL, ALCHEMICAL TREATISES
fol. 115 *Alchemical Diagram*

On this page Lull is shown at the top in the center: *Ego sum rerum naturalium doctor.* Some of Lull's genuine works use diagrams as aids to comprehension and this practice is adopted here.

The full-page and the numerous smaller miniatures in the manuscript are by Girolamo da Cremona, to whom they were already attributed by Milanesi in 1850. Girolamo di Giovanni de'Corradi da Cremona is first heard of in a letter from Barbara of Brandenburg, Marchesa of Mantua, on November 10, 1461, in which she says that she has instructed Mantegna to come to an agreement with a young man *di questa terra,* (of this region), for the illumination of a Missal. She also says she will not employ Belbello (da Pavia) any more. The Missal with illumination by the two artists still survives at Mantua. From 1468 to 1474 Girolamo was receiving payments for illustrations in the great *corali* of Siena Cathedral. A Breviary written for the Hospital of Sta. Maria Nuova, Florence by the priest Giuliano da Firenze in 1473, with illumination by Girolamo and other artists, shows he was working in Florence at this time. In January 1475 and June 1476, Girolamo was in Venice where he was at work on a Missal for Lucrezia dei Medici. For his Venetian period see Plates 17–18. Girolamo's early style (Plate 22) clearly derives from Mantegna and the Paduan school. While working in Siena under the influence of his close collaboration with Liberale da Verona there is a change to more vigorous compositions with restless, animated figures. The present manuscript is not dated but probably belongs to the same period as the Florentine Breviary, c. 1474.

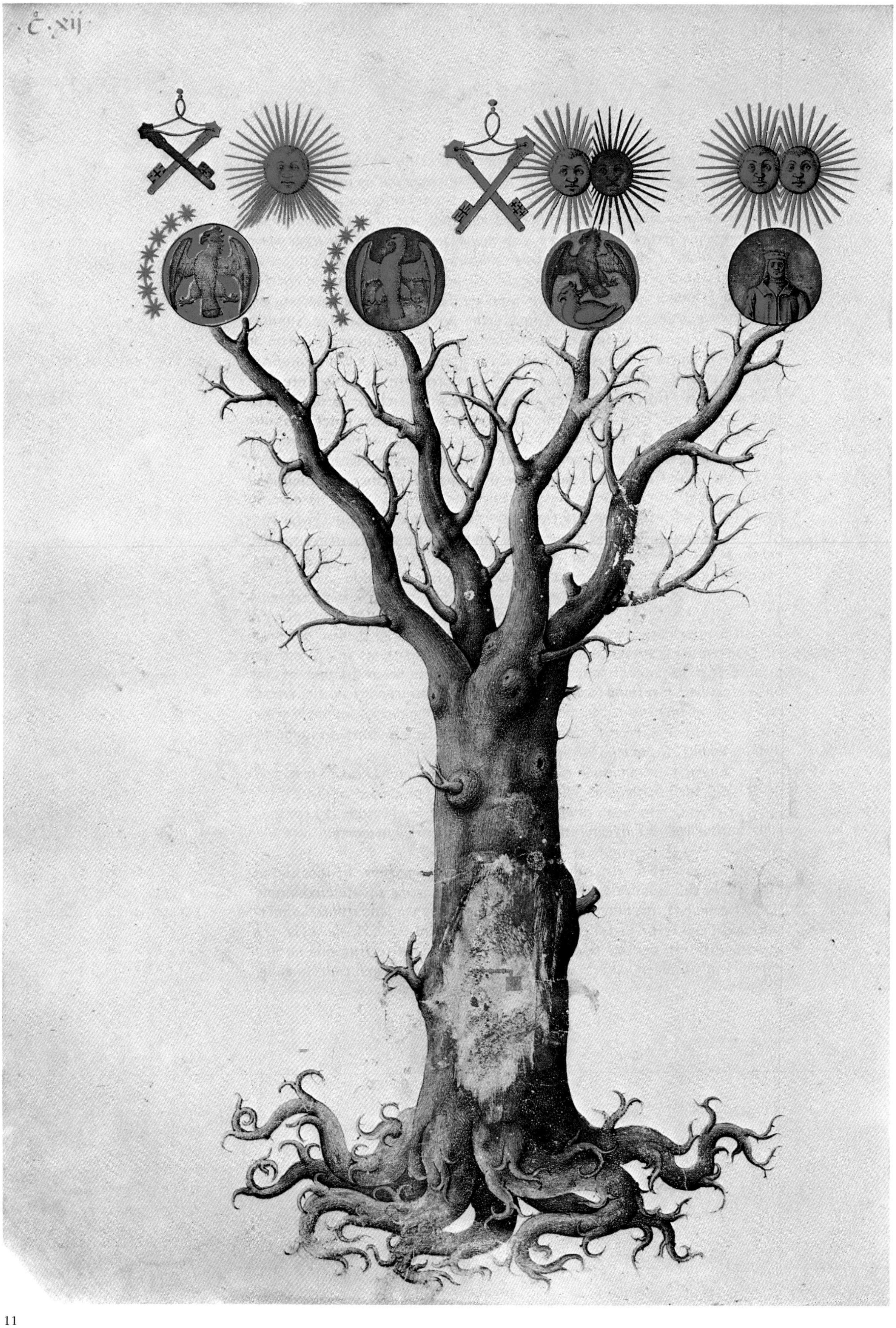


11

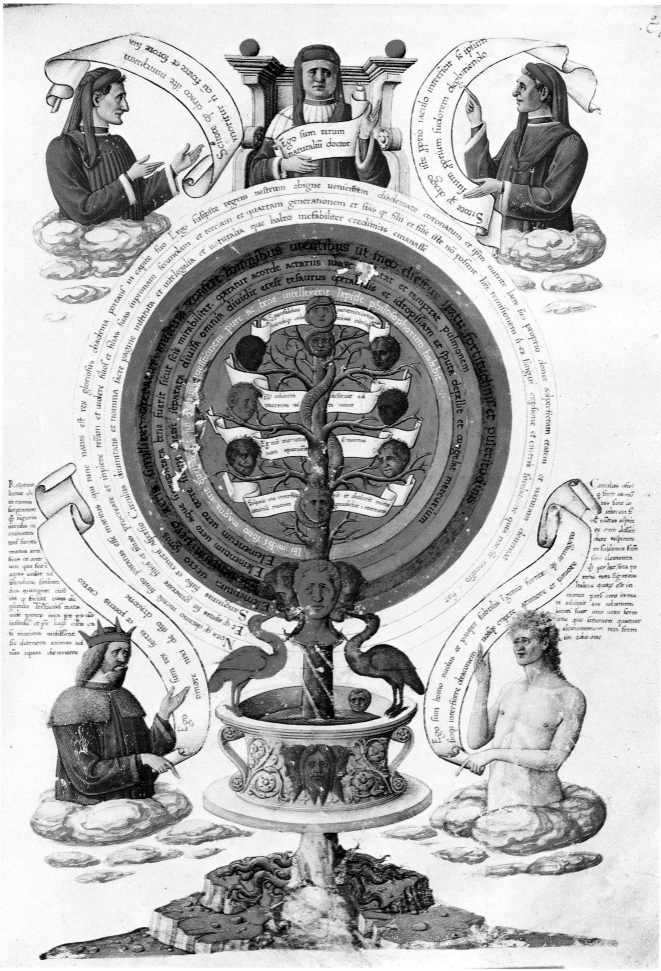

12

## PLATE 13

S<small>UETONIUS</small>, L<small>IVES OF THE</small> T<small>WELVE</small> C<small>AESARS</small>
fol. 1 *Life of Julius Caesar*

Gaius Suetonius Tranquillus (75–160 A.D.) was secretary to the Emperor Hadrian. His Lives of the early Roman Emperors is the only one of his works to survive complete. It was known throughout the Middle Ages, and in the Renaissance a number of finely illuminated copies were made.

The colored epigraphic capitals on this page and the fine Italic script of the text are attributable to the Paduan scribe Bartolomeo Sanvito (1435–after 1518), who was first identified by James Wardrop. The artist, who also illuminated a number of other manuscripts written by Sanvito mostly in Rome in the late 1470s and the 1480s (Figure 14), shows clearly his dependence on the Paduan antiquarian tradition and the work of Mantegna. It has been suggested that he was Sanvito himself. Another possibility, since he was clearly a professional artist with great gifts, is that he is to be identified with another Paduan, Lauro Padovano, by whom we have some apparently documented paintings and who is mentioned by Sanvito in his journal.

The frontispiece is composed of classical trophies supported by two carved drums. The motif of the *putto* in a mask on the left is also found in a Eusebius written by Sanvito and illuminated by the same artist for Bernardo Bembo. The title is written as if it were on a sheet suspended in the center. Two winged females, based on a classical statue of the type of the winged Victory of Brescia, inscribe shields on either side of the capital *A*. This letter is faceted as if three-dimensional. The antiquary and friend of Mantegna, Felice Feliano, wrote the earliest treatise we have on the design of such letters based on classical sources. Similar initials are to be found in a number of Paduan manuscripts, and Mantegna himself uses Roman epigraphic capitals in his paintings.

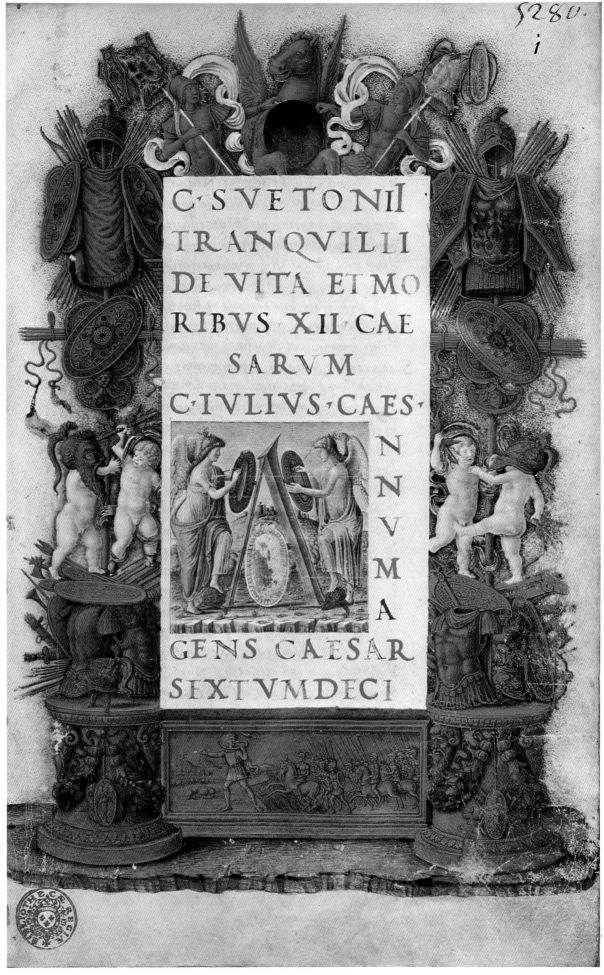

C·SVETONII
TRANQVILLI
DE VITA ET MO
RIBVS XII CAE
SARVM
C·IVLIVS·CAES·
GENS CAESAR
SEXTVMDECI

ANNVMA

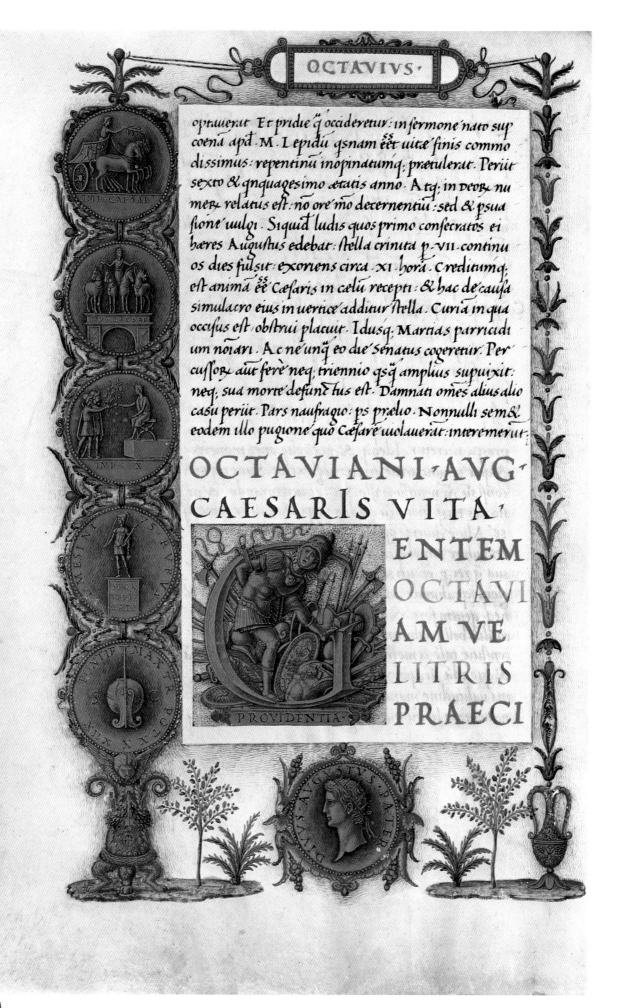

optauerat. Et pridie q̃ occideretur: in sermone nato sup
coenā apd .M. Lepidū qsnam ēēt uitæ finis commo
dissimus: repentinū inopinatumq̃. prætulerat. Periit
sexto & q̃nquagesimo ætatis anno. Atq̃. in Deoꝛ. nu
meꝝ relatus est. no ore ꝙ̃ mo decernentiū: sed & psua
sione uulgi. Siquid ludis quos primo consecratos ei
hæres Augustus edebat: stella crinita p̃·VII·continu
os dies fulsit: exoriens circa·XI·horā. Creditumq̃.
est animā ēē Cæsaris in cælū recepti: & hac de causa
simulacro eius in uertice additur stella. Curia in qua
occisus est/obstrui placuit. Idusq̃. Martias parricidi
um notari. Ac ne unq̃ eo die Senatus cogeretur. Per
cussoꝝ aut ferè neq̃ triennio qsq̃ amplius supuixit:
neq̃ sua morte defunctus est. Damnati omēs alius alio
casu periit. Pars naufragio: ps prælio. Nonnulli sem &
eodem illo pugione quo Cæsarē uiolauerat: interemerut.

# OCTAVIANI·AVG·
# CAESARIS VITA·
# ENTEM
# OCTAVI
# AM VE
# LITRIS
# PRÆCI

PROVIDENTIA·

DIVVS·AVGVSTVS·PATER·

## PLATE 14

SUETONIUS, LIVES OF THE TWELVE CAESARS
fol. 22v *Life of Octavian*

This page shows the beginning of the life of Octavian, later Augustus. In the faceted initial *G* is an armed soldier and the motto 'Providentia.' In the lower margin is a copy of a commemorative coin with the head of Augustus issued by Tiberius. This idea of illustrating the Lives of Roman Emperors with authentic coin portraits connects up both with the beginnings of the formation in the Renaissance of cabinets of antique coins and with the development of the bronze medal as one of the great Renaissance art forms. The idea may have originated with the painter and medallist Pisanello (d. 1455/6). A mid-fifteenth-century manuscript of the *Historia Augusta,* a text containing lives of later Roman Emperors, now in Turin, contains coin-type portraits and has been ascribed to him. It was made for Lodovico Gonzaga, Marquis of Mantua, and in 1466 his son, Cardinal Francesco, wrote from Rome asking for the loan of such a manuscript, since he wanted to have the portraits copied and could find no other copy containing them.

A copy of the *Historia Augusta* written by Sanvito and illuminated by the present artist survives, but the original owner is not known. The arms in the present manuscript on folio 1 are also erased, but both manuscripts might well have been written for the Cardinal, since he was the patron of Sanvito (Figure 14). Another Suetonius written by Sanvito for another member of the same circle, Ludovico Agneli, bishop of Mantua, has similar illumination.

The other coins in the left margin are all recognizable issues of Augustus or, on the lower left, the rudder and globe, Tiberius (cf. H. Mattingly, *Coins of the Roman Empire in the British Museum,* I, London 1923, Plates 3, 10, 15, 25).

## PLATE 15

JOHANNES DE DEO (?), COLUMBA
fol. III *Frontispiece, Book I*

This allegorical Christian treatise is by an anonymous Carthusian monk, perhaps Johannes de Deo of S. Andrea de Littore, Venice. He sees the Holy Dove
(*columba*) as the symbol of all the Christian virtues. The frontispiece to Book
I shows the Dove surrounded by the Seven Virtues. Below are the four cardinal
virtues, Courage with a column, Prudence with a mirror, Justice with a sword,
and Temperance pouring water from one vase to another. Above, supporting
the canopy, are the three theological virtues, Hope with an anchor, Charity
pouring gold coins from a purse, and Faith with a chalice at her feet.

On the two friezes below are represented scenes from the Life of Saint Bruno
(c. 1032–1101), founder of the Carthusian order. Above is the story of the
Canon of Notre Dame, who, after his death and during the burial service,
miraculously cried out that he had been called to the Judgment of God and
justly condemned. This so impressed Saint Bruno that he resolved to retire to
a monastery. Below is the dream of Saint Hugh of Grenoble, who saw seven
stars signifying Saint Bruno and his six companions. They later founded the
Chartreuse in the mountains near Grenoble under the bishop's protection.

There are good grounds for identifying the illuminator of this page with
Antonio Maria Sforza (d. 1519) whose documented works are in two incun-
ables of 1491 and 1497. This manuscript belongs to an earlier period and is
probably contemporary with a Breviary illuminated by him, which was written
in 1473.

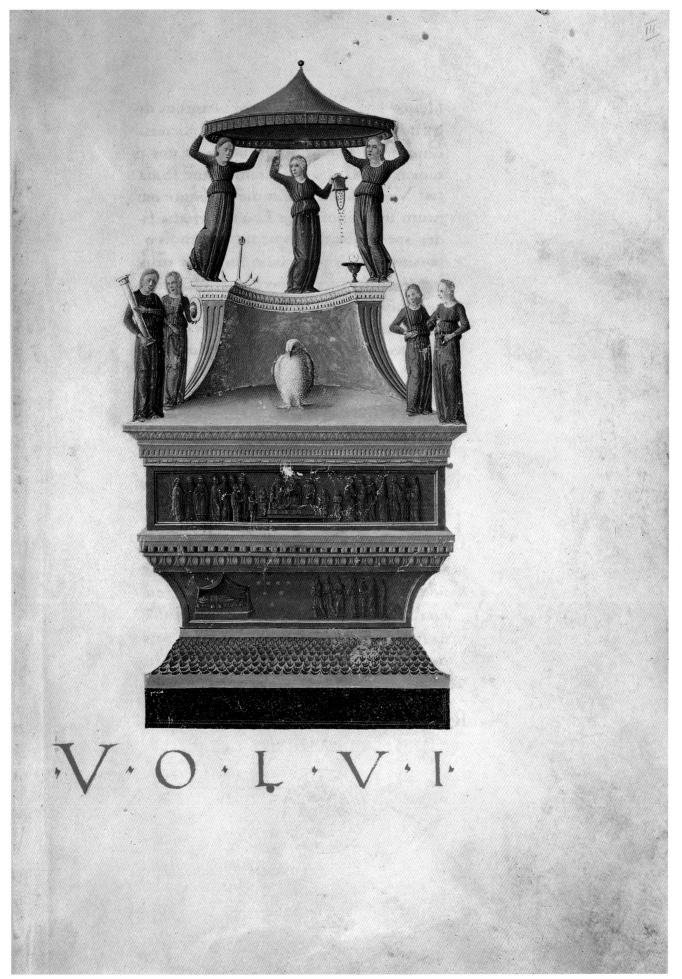

· V · O · L · V · I ·

## PLATE 16

JOHANNES DE DEO (?), COLUMBA
fol. 43 *Frontispiece, Book II*

The treatise is divided into three books and this is the title-page of the third book. We see another experiment in the creation of an architectural frontispiece. The artist has made it look as if a torn piece of parchment has been suspended in front of the structure with the first words of the book *Hoc et enim* written on it. A loggia opens in the center with a view through to a landscape. Above, two *putti* support a blank disc on which it was probably intended a title or rubric should be written.

The illumination has been attributed to the so-called 'Maestro dei Putti,' an illuminator working in Padua or Venice in the 1470s and 1480s. Although he certainly executed the frontispiece to Book III, part 2, which bears what seems to be his motto in Greek, the present miniature and the frontispiece to Book II seem to be by a third hand. In addition to these frontispieces there are many historiated initials by the 'Maestro dei Putti' and Antonio Maria Sforza.

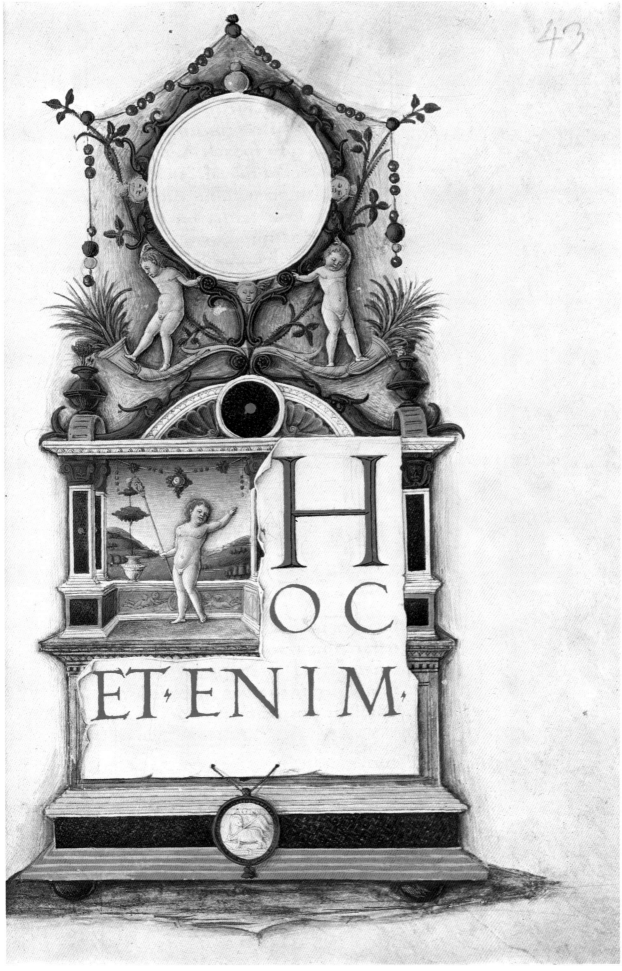

PLATE 17

Aristotle, Works
*Frontispiece to Volume I*

This is not a manuscript but an *incunabulum*, that is a book printed before 1500 A.D. It is included here both because of its superb illumination and to make the point that the introduction of printing did not immediately spell the end of illumination by hand. This edition of Aristotle's works in Latin translation was printed at Venice in 1483 by Andrea Torresani and Bartholomaeus de Blavis, and this particular copy is a *de luxe* production printed on vellum and specially illuminated for Peter Ugelheimer. Ugelheimer, a German merchant from Ulm, had put capital into the printing firm of Nicholas Jenson, which after Jenson's death was taken over by Torresani. Other splendid vellum copies of books printed by Jenson and illuminated for Ugelheimer are at Gotha today. This is the frontispiece to the first volume and below the text can be read the inscription: *Ulmer Aristotelem Petrus produxeat orbi.*

The page is shown in *trompe l'oeil* as if we could see through its torn holes and past its curling edges. Below are classical fauns (one carries a basket and is a copy of a famous pair of antique statues, the Barberini fauns), and *putti*. Above, Aristotle and another philosopher are seen in dispute. The book belonged to Henry Yates Thompson (Plates 6, 7, 38, 39), before its acquisition by the Morgan Library.

## PLATE 18

ARISTOTLE, WORKS
*Frontispiece to Volume II*

In this miniature the page is painted to be seen as if the block of print is hanging from a balcony on which stand a group of philosophers. To the right there is a monkey on the balustrade. Below, a faun is piping accompanied by a *putto,* deer and rabbits. To the right we see through to a distant landscape.

The illumination of the two frontispieces has been attributed to Girolamo da Cremona (Plates 11–12) who is known to have been in Venice in 1475–76, and also to Jacometto Veneziano, by whom we have two apparently documented portraits now in the Lehmann Collection at the Metropolitan Museum in New York. Jacometto is known to have been an illuminator. Several other manuscripts and printed books with a Venetian provenance and of the same period are certainly by the same artist as the Aristotle. If he is really Girolamo, then he had again developed considerably by contact with other artists. His style had become softer and more luminous and this would be due to the effect on him of such Venetian paintings as Giovanni Bellini's Resurrection of c. 1475–79 (which is now in Berlin). Another Venetian feature is the inclusion of the turbanned oriental figures. Gentile Bellini, Giovanni's brother, was sent as official state painter to Constantinople in 1479 at the Sultan's request, and returned in 1481.

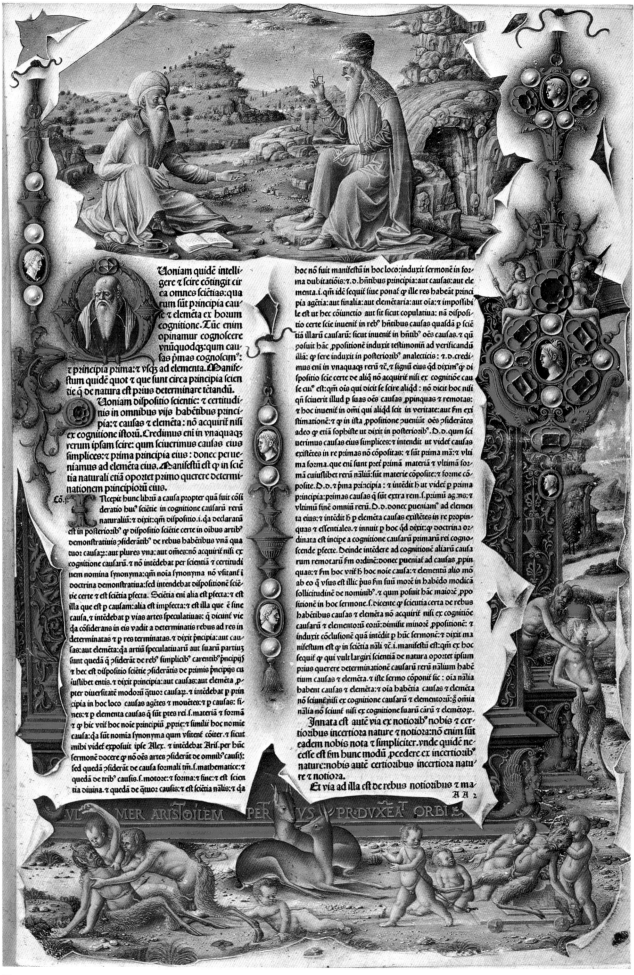

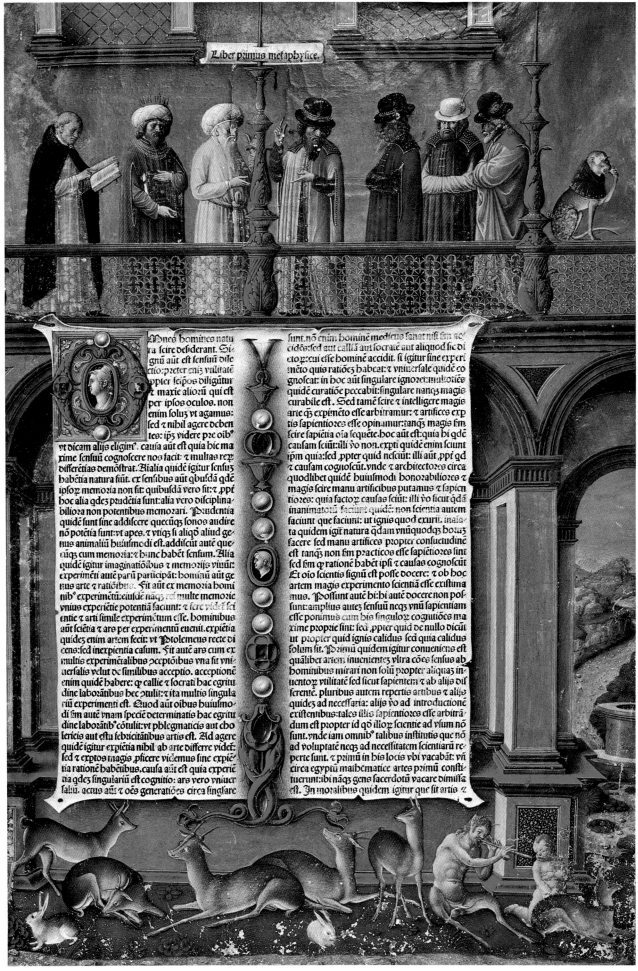

PLATES 19–20

BIBLE OF BORSO D'ESTE. VOLUME I
fol. 5v & fol. *6 Book of Genesis, Volume I*

This Bible in two volumes was commissioned by Borso d'Este (born 1413) who had succeeded his brother Lionello as lord of Ferrara in 1450. In 1452 he was given the title of Duke of Modena and Reggio by the Emperor Frederick III, and in 1471 he was made Duke of Ferrara by Pope Paul II. He died on August 19 the same year. He built up an important library which he made accessible to scholars at the University of Ferrara, amongst whom was Guarino of Verona (d. 1460), and he was a notable patron both of literature and art. Roger van der Weyden and Piero della Francesca were among the painters working at Ferrara during the period of his rule.

## PLATES 19-20 (Continued)

The contract for the production of the Bible between Borso's agent, Galeotto dell'Assassino, and the illuminators, Taddeo Crivelli and Franco dei Russi, is dated July 2, 1455, and the work took six years to complete. The ducal accounts give the name of the scribe, Pietro Paolo Marone, and enable us to identify a number of the artists. A *libro di dibituri e crededuri* of Crivelli also survives, in which payments from him as the main entrepreneur to his various assistants are recorded.

This opening is for the Book of Genesis. The scenes show the Creation of the Universe, of the Earth, of the birds and fishes, of the animals, of Adam and Eve, Adam naming the animals, and God showing Adam the Tree of the Knowledge of Good and Evil. In the border are Borso's arms and his emblems, among them the diamond ring, the Unicorn, and the "Paraduro," a barrier on the river Po. The illumination is by Crivelli who took the main part in the work on the Bible.

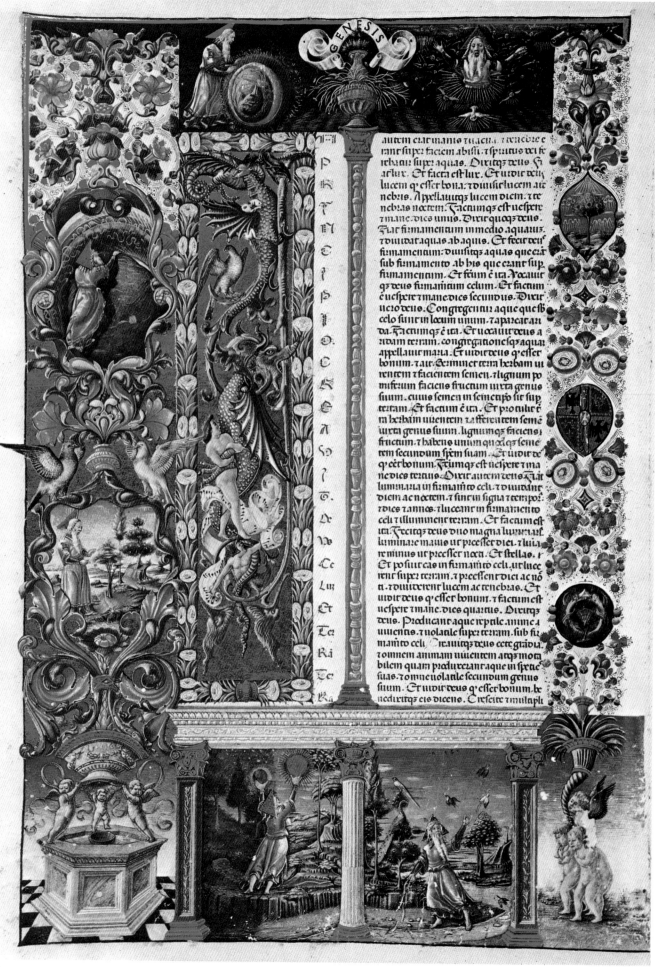

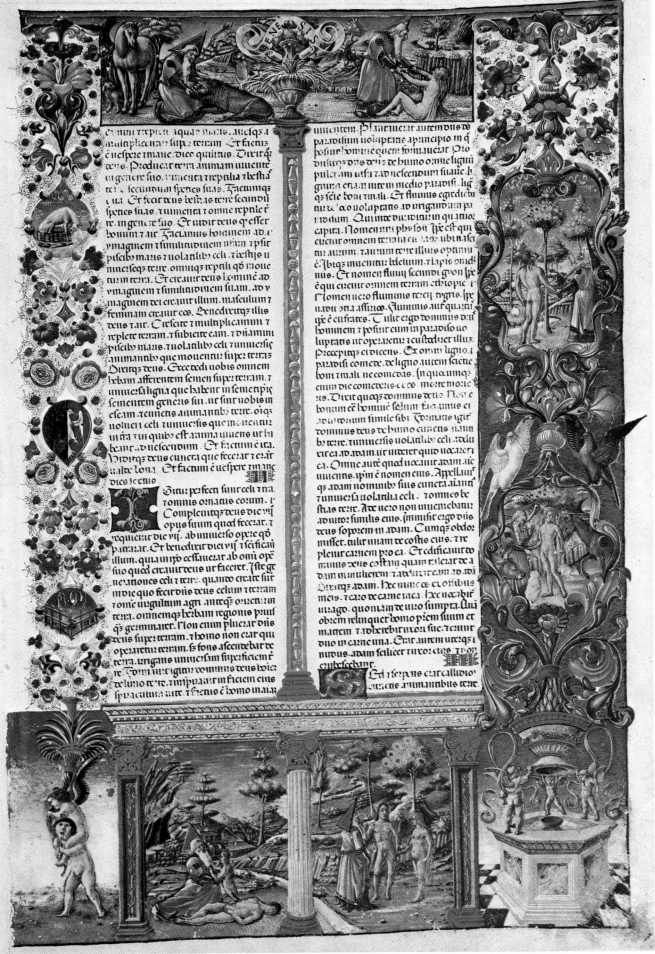

PLATE 21

BIBLE OF BORSO D'ESTE
fol. 212 *Book of Tobias, Volume I*

This is the opening of the Book of Tobias. In the initial *C* to the preface by
Saint Jerome, on the left, the saint is shown seated wearing his cardinal's hat.
In the initial *T,* on the right, the young Tobias is shown taking leave of his
parents. In the right border the old Tobias, his father, is shown clothing the
poor (Chapter I, Verse 19). The borders again contain Borso's arms and
emblems. The miniatures are by Giorgio d'Alemagna, whose name occurs
in the d'Este accounts from 1441 to 1479. His son, Martino da Modena, became
one of the leading illuminators at Ferrara in the next generation.

# PLATE 22

BIBLE OF BORSO D'ESTE
fol. 157v *Gospel of Saint Luke, Volume II*

This page, with the preface to Saint Luke's Gospel, *Lucas syrus natione,* and
the beginning of the Gospel, *Quoniam quidem,* shows the respective authors,
Saint Jerome and the Evangelist. Since the Gospel begins with an account
of the Birth of Saint John the Baptist this probably is the scene represented
below. It might, however, be the Nativity of the Virgin Mary, since it is
flanked by the Annunciation, the angel Gabriel kneeling on the left and the
Virgin on the right. In the initial *F* is the scene of the angel foretelling the
Baptist's birth to his father, Zacharias. The illumination of this page has been
attributed to Marco dell' Avogaro whose name suggests he was Venetian, on
the basis of payments in the accounts. The style, however, seems indistinguish-
able from that of Girolamo da Cremona (Plates 11–12) and recently this and
other pages have been attributed to him.

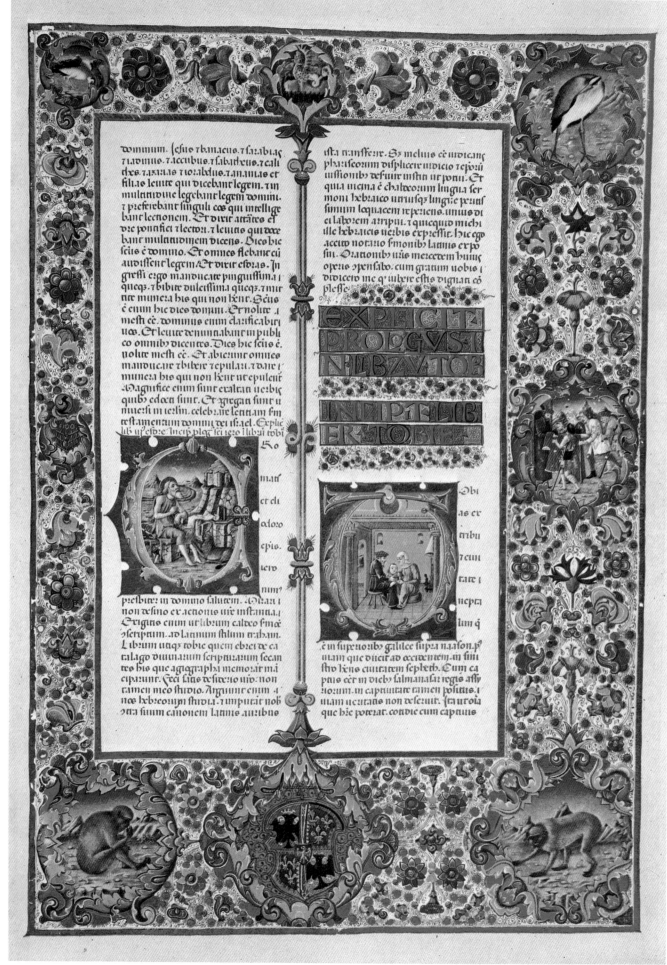

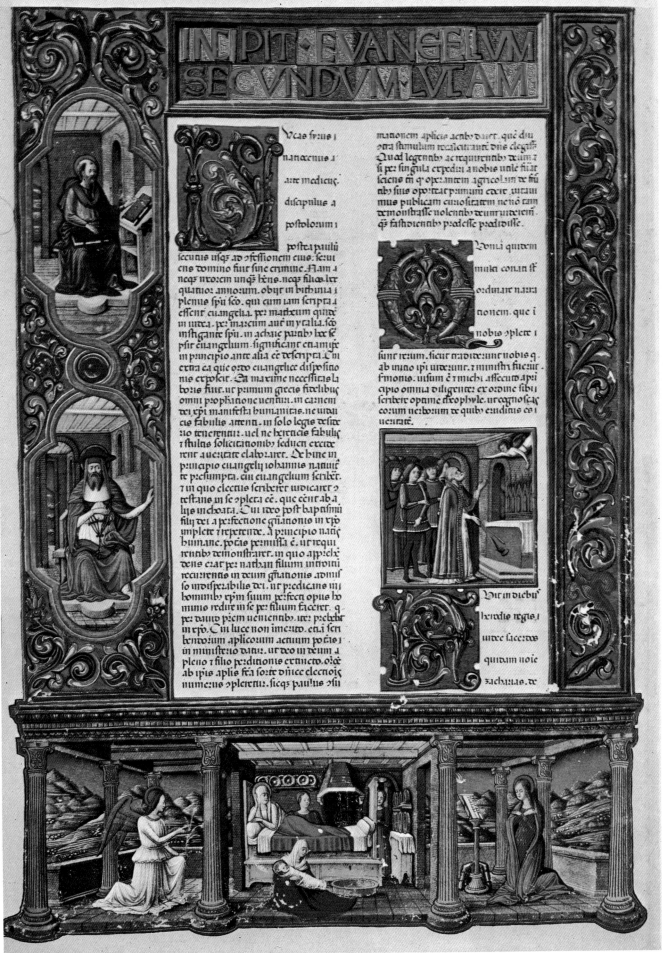

22

PLATE 23

FEDERIGO DA MONTEFELTRO'S DANTE, LA DIVINA COMMEDIA
fol. 1 *Inferno, Canto I*

This copy of the Divine Comedy was written for Federigo da Montefeltro by Matteo de' Contugi of Volterra probably in 1477 or early 1478. Federigo was born in 1422 and succeeded his father as lord of Urbino in 1444. From this relatively humble position he became one of the most successful of Renaissance soldiers, commanding the troops of various states as a condottiere. Pope Sixtus IV rewarded him in 1474 with the title of Duke and Papal Gonfaloniere, in virtue of which he added the cross keys and papal tiara to his arms. He devoted much of the huge profits of his campaigns to the building of his great palace at Urbino, the patronage of artists including Piero della Francesca and Justus van Ghent, and the building up of his library.

This manuscript was left incomplete at the Duke's death in 1482, and only seventy-eight miniatures were executed before then. In the early seventeenth century another forty-two were added. The main miniature of the frontispiece to *Inferno* shows Dante's meeting with the Wolf, the Leopard, and the Lion. Behind him is his rescuer, Virgil. In the margin to the right and below, inserted in the white-vine border, are medallions showing Dante dreaming, his meetings with the Leopard and the Lion, and finally Virgil's meeting with Beatrice in Limbo. Federigo's arms are in the center below, and above are three *putti* playing with the Garter awarded to Federigo by Edward IV of England in 1474. There are also animal studies in the border to the left and above, including the Ermine, emblem of the chivalric order of Naples, of which Ferrante I made Federigo a member, also in 1474. The miniature is by Guglielmo Giraldi.

## PLATE 24

FEDERIGO DA MONTEFELTRO'S DANTE, LA DIVINA COMMEDIA
fol. 20 *Inferno, Canto VIII*

This miniature prefaces *Inferno,* Canto VIII. We see the watchtower on the left sending a beacon signal to the city of Dis. As Dante and Virgil are ferried across the Styx by the boatman Phlegyas, they encounter Filippo Argenti, one of the wrathful, who tries to attack them. In the distance Dante and Virgil are shown again, parleying with the fallen Angels who garrison the flaming city. The miniatures in this manuscript are not placed in the lower margin as in King Alfonso's Dante (Plates 6–7). Instead they preface each Canto.

This miniature is also by Guglielmo Giraldi, who worked mainly at Ferrara for the D'Este. His earliest surviving work is an Aulus Gellius signed and dated 1448. In October 1478 Matteo de' Contugi wrote to Federigo Gonzaga at Mantua to say that he had gone to Ferrara to see about the illumination of various manuscripts for Federigo including the Dante, for which the cost of the illumination was three hundred and ten ducats. In December 1480 Federigo wrote to the Duke of Ferrara asking permission for Giraldi to come to Urbino to finish the work. Giraldi was assisted by his nephew Alessandro Leoni, and another illuminator.

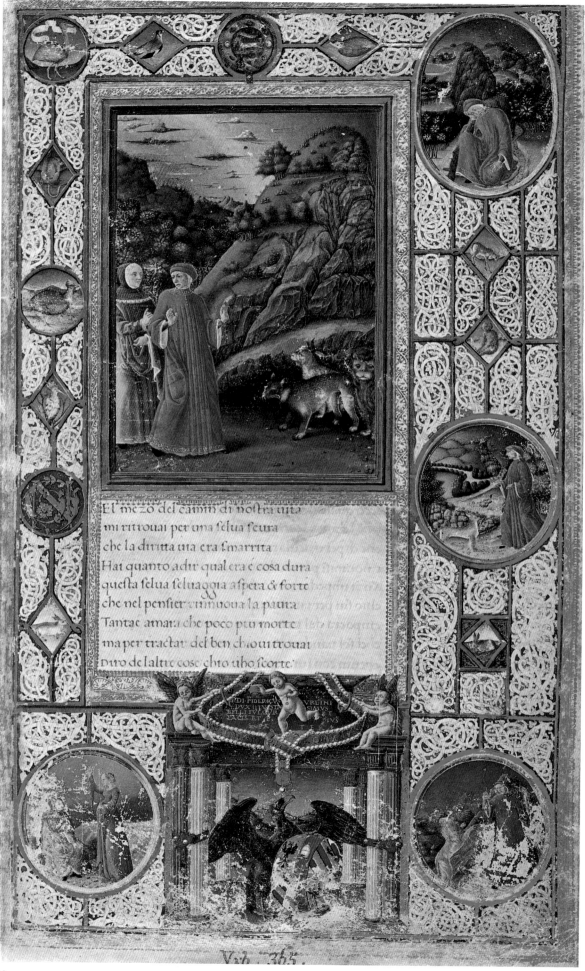

El mezo del camin di nostra uita
mi ritrouai per una selua scura
che la diritta uia era smarrita
Hai quanto adir qual era e cosa dura
questa selua seluaggia aspera & forte
che nel pensier rinnoua la paura
Tantae amara che poco piu morte
ma per tractar del ben chioui trouai
Diro de laltre cose chio uho scorte

23

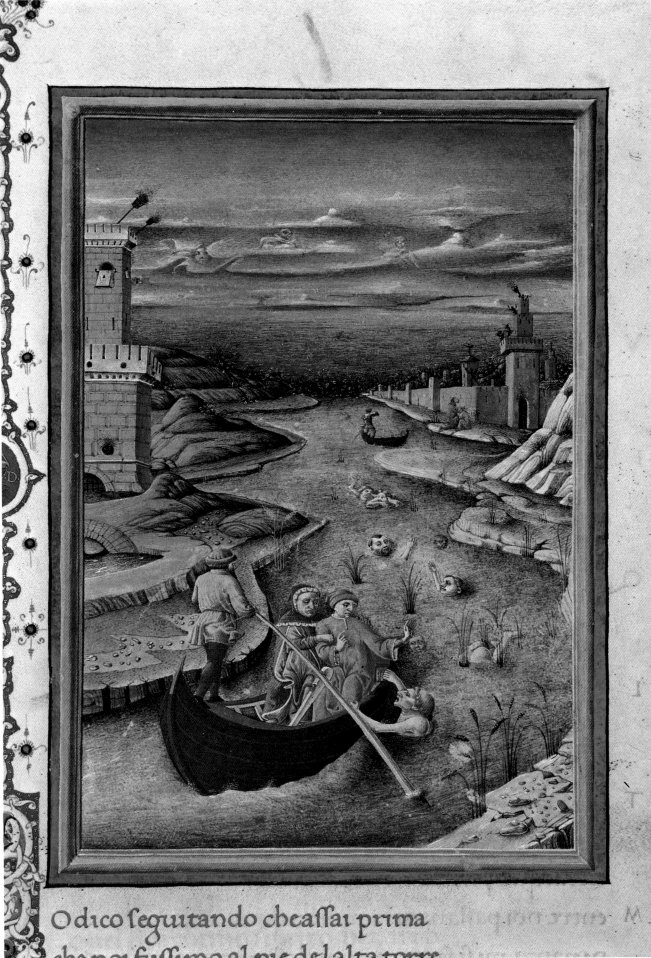

O dico feguitando cheaffai prima

24

PLATE 25

FEDERIGO DA MONTEFELTRO'S DANTE, LA DIVINA COMMEDIA
fol. 97 *Purgatorio, Canto I*

The frontispiece to *Purgatorio* is also decorated with a sumptuous border partly of white-vine, partly of blue interlace on gold. The main miniature is seen through a triumphal arch and shows the meeting of Virgil and Dante with Cato, the guardian of the Mountain. The three border medallions show Dante bathing his hands in the dew of the meadow (lines 121–25), Virgil wiping away the tears from his face (lines 126–29), and Virgil and Dante on the shore of the sea with the mountain of Purgatory behind them. This miniature is also by Giraldi.

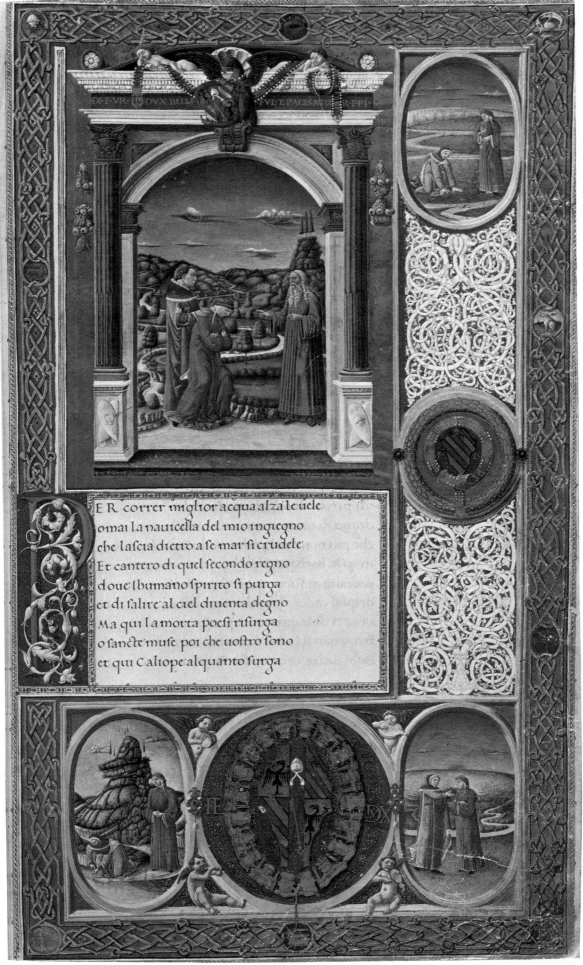

PER correr miglior acqua alza le uele
omai la nauicella del mio ingiegno
che lascia dietro a se mar si crudele
Et cantero di quel secondo regno
doue lhumano spirito si purga
et di salire al ciel diuenta degno
Ma qui la morta poesi risurga
o sancte muse poi che uostro sono
et qui Caliope alquanto surga

PLATE 26

FEDERIGO DA MONTEFELTRO'S DANTE, LA DIVINA COMMEDIA
fol. 127 *Purgatorio, Canto XIII*

This miniature illustrates *Purgatorio,* Cantos X-XII. Dante and Virgil examine the third of the reliefs set up as examples of Humility to the Proud. It shows the Emperor Trajan about to set out on a campaign, delaying to give justice to a widow whose son has been killed. Below, the Proud crouch, each weighed down by a huge stone. Canto XI contains the famous passage concerning Oderisi da Gubbio, the illuminator, who is surpassed by Franco Bolognese, just as Giotto has surpassed Cimabue.

This miniature has been attributed to Franco dei Russi who is first heard of at Ferrara in connection with the Bible of Borso d'Este in 1453 (Plates 19–22). He is documented at the court of Urbino at this time, where he also illuminated a number of other manuscripts for Federigo. It is not clear if he was collaborating with Giraldi or if he had taken over the commission. He has represented the carving described by Dante as a classical relief *al antica.*

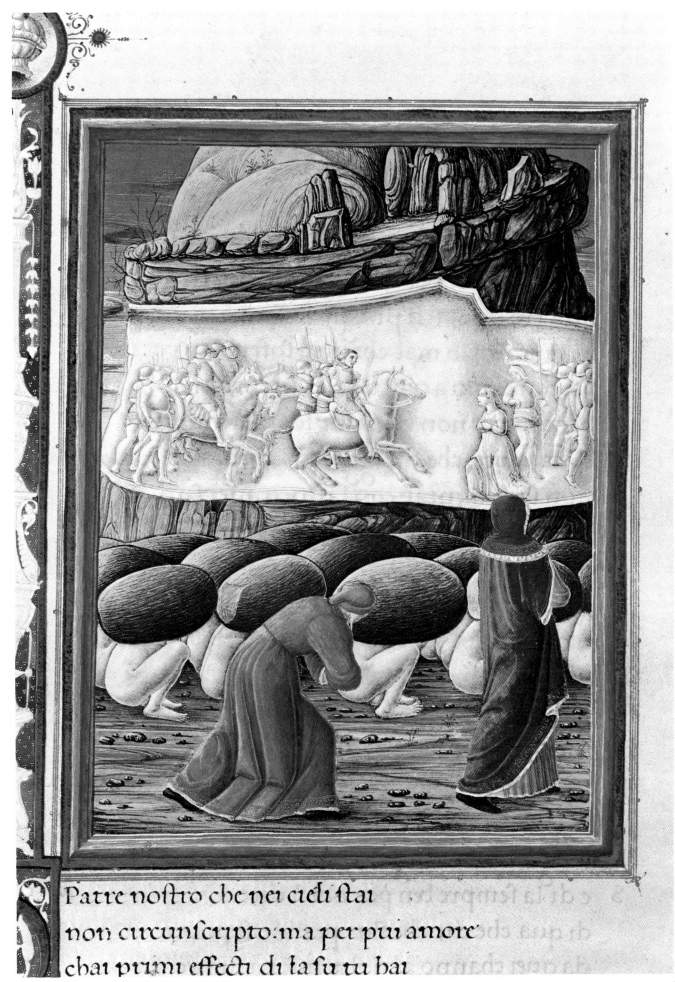

Patre nostro che nei cieli stai
non circunscripto:ma per piu amore
chai primi effecti di lasu tu hai

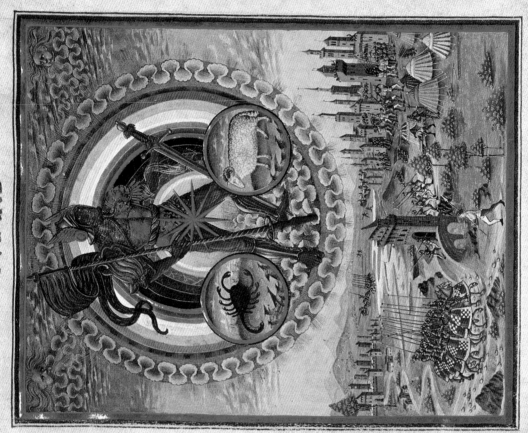

· MARS ·

Il bellicoso marte sempre infiama
Li animi altrui al guerreggiare et ffessa
Pez quello: quello ne sana sua brama

27 a

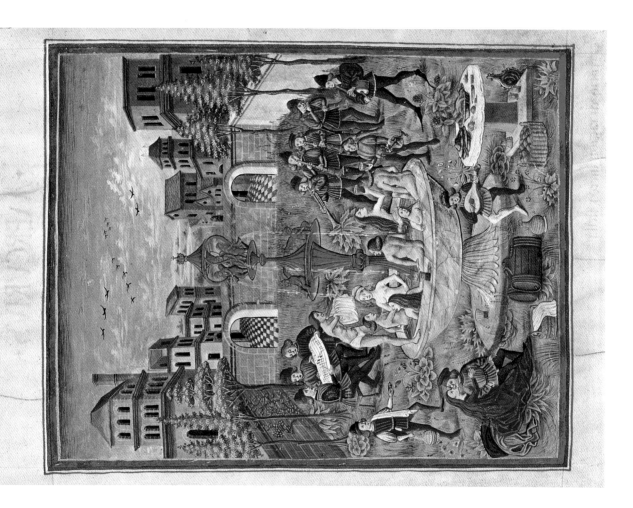

27 b

PLATE 27

DE SPHERA
a) fol. 7v *The Planet Mars*
b) fol. 10 *The Fountain of Youth*

This little manuscript contains a number of astrological and astronomical diagrams and fourteen full-page miniatures of the seven Planets and their "children," that is those born under their influence and whose character and destiny they were thought to mold. Although often condemned by the Church, the popularity and influence of such speculations continued throughout the Middle Ages and into the Renaissance and, like Hitler, many Renaissance tyrants kept their own astrologer to advise them on the propitious times for their actions.

Medieval astrology was based in large part on Latin texts of the Classical and Late Antique periods, which themselves owed much to Greek and Eastern sources. The iconography of the representations of the planets and constellations can also be traced back via the medieval copies to the Classical period.

Folio 7v (a). Here we see the fiery Planet, Mars, God of War in the Roman Pantheon, with sword, shield and banner and flanked by the Zodiac signs, Scorpio and Aries (the Ram). Below a city is being besieged.

Folio 10 (b). Here we see the children of Venus bathing in the Fountain of Youth. The fountain with four couples in it is in a walled garden in a city with a view beyond into the country. Music, "the food of Love," is represented by a trio singing on the left and a band of wind players on the right. On a table a picnic with plenty of wine is laid out. The Greek writer Pausanias speaks of a fountain in which the Goddess Juno bathed to retain her youth. The idea is taken up in medieval romances and frequently illustrated in the later Middle Ages.

## PLATE 28

DE SPHERA
fol. 11 *Those Born Under the Planet Mercury*

This page shows the children of the Planet Mercury, patron of artists and craftsmen. In the center two cooks are preparing food for the meal taking place at the top. On the left we see, below, the armorers with completed breast plates, etc., hanging above their heads; the clockmakers in the center; a scribe writing, above; and on the right, above, a painter working on a panel; a sculptor in the center; and, below, an organ-maker.

On folio 4 are the arms and emblems of Francesco Sforza and his wife, Bianca, daughter of Filippo Maria Visconti, Duke of Milan. They married in 1441 and Francesco succeeded his father-in-law as Duke in 1450 after a period in which Milan was a republic (Plate 8). The *De Sphera* is included in the seventeenth-century library catalogue of the D'Este of Ferrara, but not in that of 1495. It is possible that it was brought to Ferrara as a result of the marriage of Anna Sforza to Alfonso I D'Este in 1491.

The miniatures still show the strong Gothic trend of Lombard illumination, though there are certain Renaissance motifs. They have been connected with Cristoforo dei Predis (Plate 30), whose signed works are of the 1470s. However, the manuscript must be before Francesco Sforza's death in 1466, and the illumination is more probably the work of a predecessor of Cristoforo's. He builds up his scenes like a tapestry landscape, without any diminution for the figures in the distance and with other disconcerting changes of scale. This also indicates an early dating in the 1450s to early 1460s. The artist's great gift is for lively observation of everyday activities.

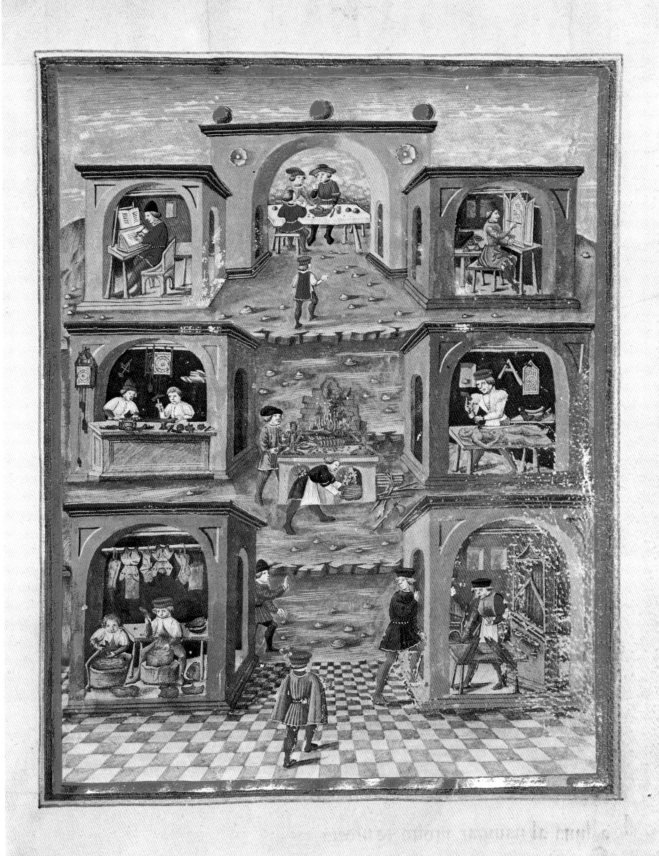

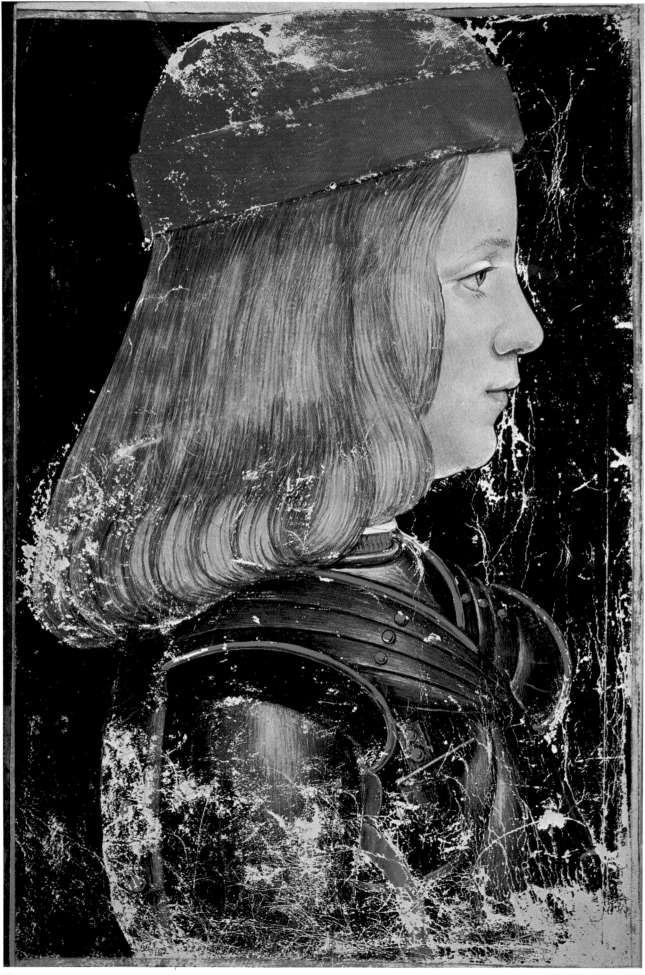

## PLATE 29

### Moral and Grammatical Texts
fol. 1v *Maximilian Sforza*

This manuscript was made for the young Maximilian Sforza, son of Lodovico il Moro, Duke of Milan, and of Beatrice d'Este. He was born in 1493 and the manuscript must have been made c. 1496–99 before the capture of the Duchy by the French in 1499–1500. A companion manuscript for the young prince, *Il libro del Jesus* (Trivulziana Cod. 2163), shows his meeting with the Emperor Maximilian in 1496.

The texts are grammatical and moral treatises suitable for the education of a young prince. The portrait has been attributed to Ambrogio de Predis, who was court painter of Lodovico il Moro from at least 1482. In April 1483, Leonardo da Vinci was staying in his home and he and his brother, Evangelista, are named as Leonardo's collaborators.

Another portrait at the end of the manuscript, folio 52v, is of Lodovico. He had seized power as regent for his nephew, the young Duke Gian Galeazzo, in 1479/80 and on Gian Galeazzo's death in 1494 had made himself duke. Lodovico, however, was captured by the French in 1500 and died in France at the château of Loches in 1508. Maximilian briefly recovered the duchy with the help of the Swiss from 1512 until 1515 when Francis I of France reconquered it. Maximilian died in 1530.

singulariter profertur.

Cuius numeri pluralis quare quia o
pluraliter profertur:

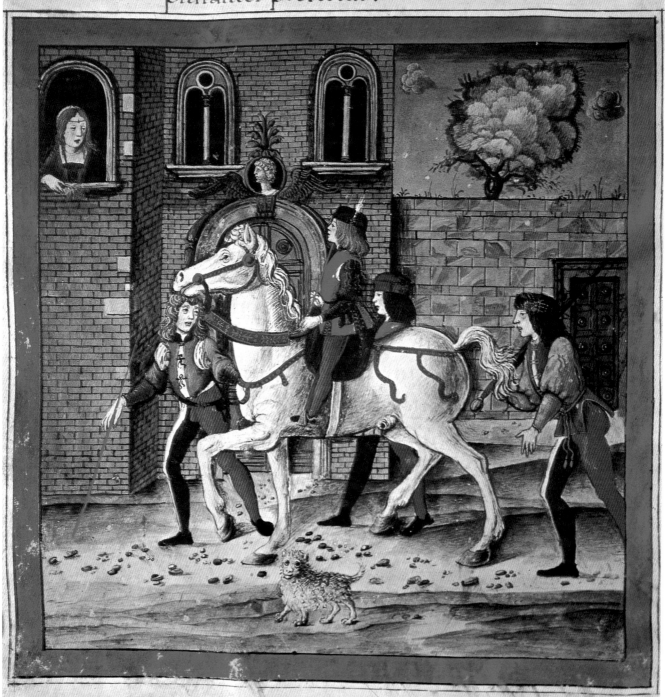

Va per milano el conte inamorato
E da tutte le dame é contemplato.

passiuo: duo: que: preteriti temporis &
futuri.

Da preteriti ut amatus.
Da futuri ut amandus.

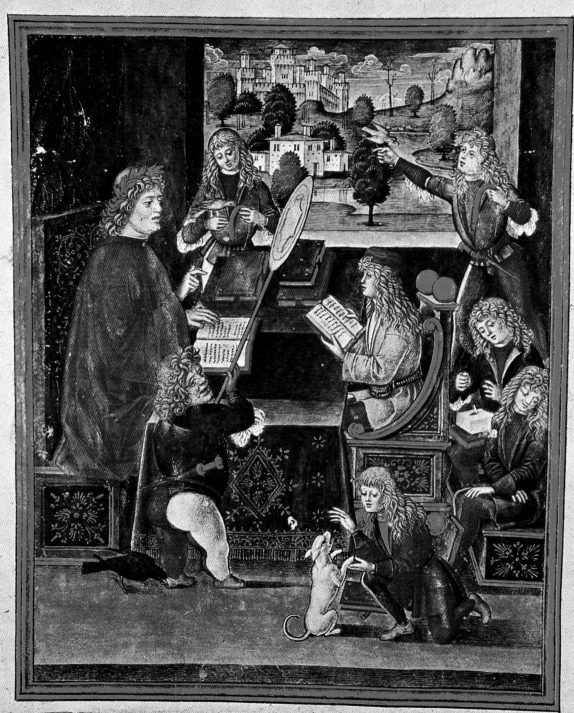

. Insin che el mastro insegna, el conte a gara.
Studia & ascolta e volunteri impara.

31

PLATE 30

MORAL AND GRAMMATICAL TREATISES
fol. 10v *Maximilian Riding Through Milan*

This miniature shows Maximilian riding through Milan accompanied by his
attendants and his dog. A lady looks out of the window of a Palazzo and the
inscription reads: "the Count (he was Count of Pavia) goes through Milan
and all the ladies watch him and are in love with him." The miniature has
been ascribed to an unknown follower of the illuminator Cristoforo de Predis,
elder brother of Ambrogio. Cristoforo himself was probably dead by 1486.

PLATE 31

<small>Moral and Grammatical Treatises</small>
fol. 13v *Maximilian At His Lessons*

Here we see Maximilian with his tutor, Gian Antonio Secco, Conte di Borella, who died in 1498. The main text of the manuscript is a Latin grammar based on the work of Aelius Donatus, the fourth-century grammarian. It is evidently a hot day, so they sit by an open window and a dwarf fans the prince. Maximilian is shown as a model pupil intent on his studies, while his less serious companions sleep or play with their pet birds or the dog. The miniature is by Gian Pietro Birago, who signed miniatures in *corali* in Brescia of 1471–73 and the printed copy of the *Sforziad* of 1494–96 in Warsaw.

## PLATE 32

MORAL AND GRAMMATICAL TREATISES
fol. 29 *Maximilian In Triumph*

The inscription reads: "the Count has subjugated all the world so he rides in triumph in this pleasant chariot." Trumpeters blow a fanfare, one of his companions brandishes a rattle, and the dwarf beats a drum while the little dog barks. The standard of the Visconti Sforza blows in the wind. Maximilian sits holding the *caduceus* of the God Mercury as a symbol of classical learning. This miniature too is by Birago, and in it he has successfully conveyed an impression of loud noise by visual means.

There are three other miniatures in the book not reproduced here, an *al fresco* meal in a garden (fol. 26), Maximilian choosing Virtue in preference to Vice (fol. 42v), and Maximilian receiving a book from his tutor (fol. 43). Another, now lost, was on folio 3. The miniatures give an exceptionally vivid picture of the young prince and his activities.

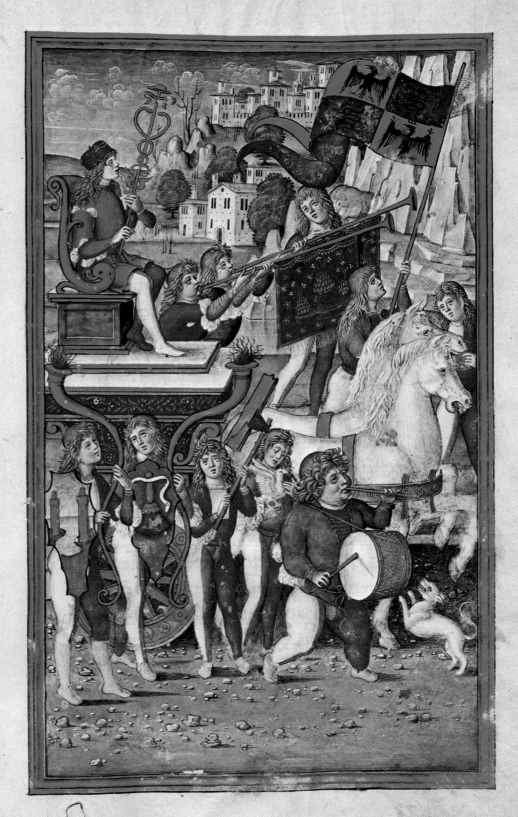

El conte ha subiugato tutto el mondo
Pero triompha in que carro iocondo

PLATE 33

CICERO, ORATIONS
fol. IIIv *King Ferrante On Horseback*

This manuscript of Cicero's Orations was written for Ferrante I of Aragon, King of Naples (1458–94). On a fly-leaf is a portrait of the king on horseback. Painted in gold on purple parchment, it is made to look like a painted equestrian monument such as the wall paintings in Florence Cathedral by Ucello of John Hawkwood and by Castagno of Niccolò da Tolentino. The inscription below, written in capitals like a classical inscription, is signed by the scribe, Joan Marco Cinico of Parma, who was employed by the kings of Naples between 1458 and 1498.

The change in style in Neapolitan illumination from Gothic to Renaissance could not be better shown than by comparing this page with the frontispiece of a Vegetius, *de re militari,* written for Alfonso of Aragon, Ferrante's father, between 1442 and 1458 (Figure XVII). There Alfonso is represented as a Gothic knight on a caparisoned horse prancing through the meadows.

## PLATE 34

CICERO, ORATIONS
fol. VI *Cicero Delivering the Pro Lege Manilia*

The opening page of the first of the orations, *Pro lege Manilia,* shows Cicero speaking in the Roman senate. It is a strange combination of classicizing motifs like the tripod on which Cicero is so uncomfortably set, with Gothic features like the vaulted hall behind. In the border are the arms of the King of Naples supported by *putti.* The initial *Q* encloses two figures shaking hands with the legend *Concordia Augusta.* This is a representation of the verso of a medal by Cristoforo di Geremia made on the occasion of the Emperor Frederic III's visit to Rome in 1469 (G. F. Hill, *Corpus of the Italian Medals of the Renaissance before Cellini,* 1930, no. 755, Plate 127), which was in turn based on early Imperial coin types.

On fol. Vv (not reproduced) the title of the work is written in epigraphic capitals on an aedicule. The illumination is by Cola Rapicano, who worked for the kings of Naples from 1451 until his death in 1488. A payment for parchment consigned to the scribe, Cinico, in 1471 *per lo Tulli del senyor Rey* may refer to this manuscript, which was acquired by Giovanni Sambuco c. 1562 and given to the future Emperor Maximilian II, King of the Romans, on May 15, 1564.

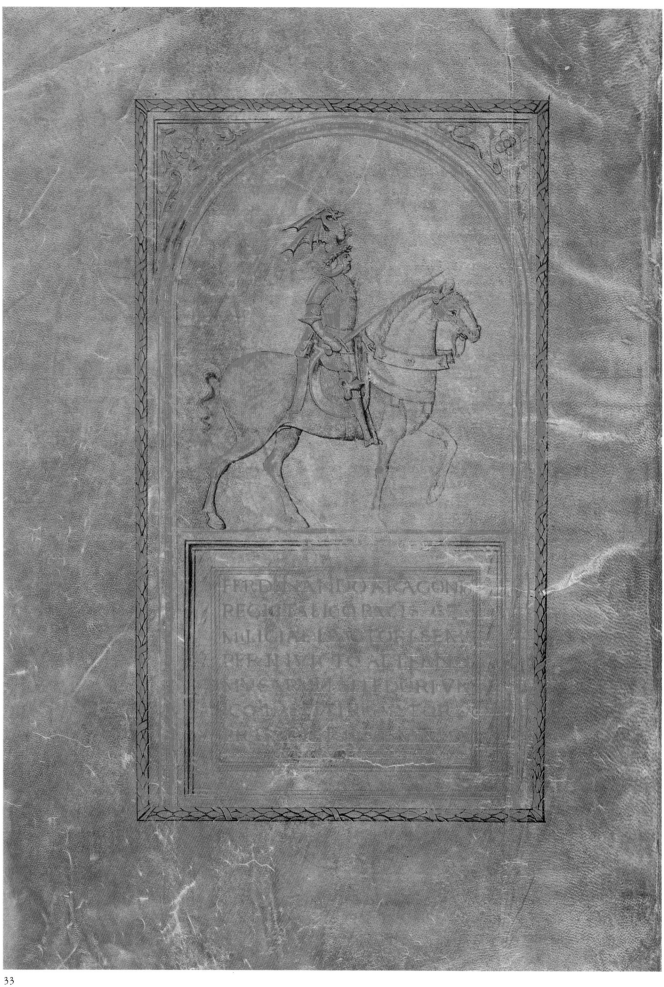

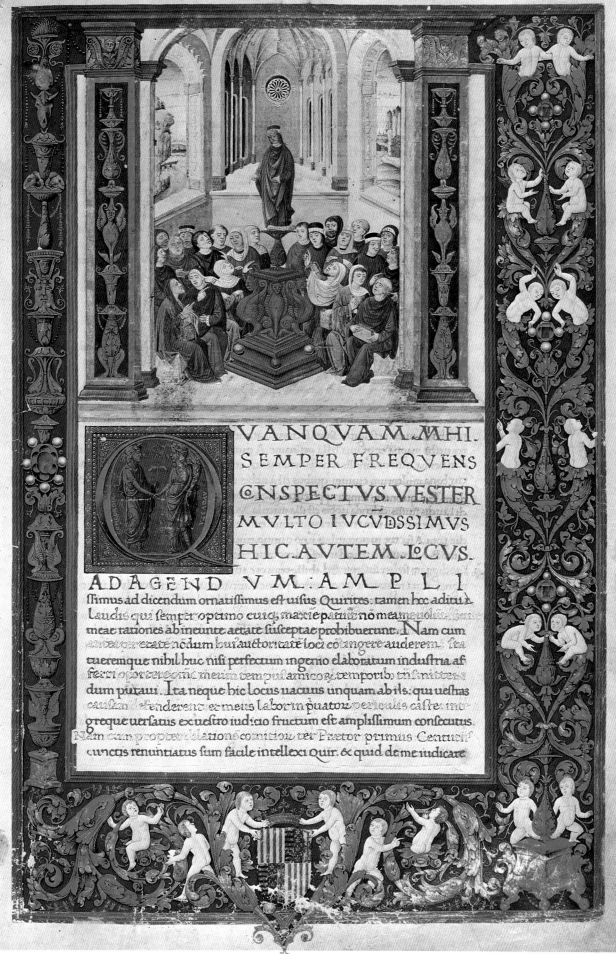

VANQVAM MIHI
SEMPER FREQVENS
CONSPECTVS VESTER
MVLTO IVCVNDISSIMVS
HIC AVTEM LOCVS.
AD AGENDVM AMPLI
ssimus ad dicendum ornatissimus est uisus Quirites. tamen hoc aditu à
Laudis qui semper optimo cuiq; maxie patuit non mea me uoluntate sed
meae rationes ab ineunte aetate susceptae prohibuerunt. Nam cum
antea per aetatem nondum huic auctoritati loci contingere auderem. Ita
tueremque nihil huc nisi perfectum ingenio elaboratum industria af
ferri oportere omne meum tempus amicorum temporibus transmitten
dum putaui. Ita neque hic locus uacuus unquam ab iis qui uestras
causam defenderent ex meus labor in puatorum periculis castre. inno
greque uersatus ex uestro iudicio fructum est amplissimum consecutus.
Nam cum propter dilationem comitiorum ter Praetor primus Centurii
cunctis renuntiatus sum facile intellexi Quir. & quid de me iudicare

# PLATE 35

ARISTOTLE, NICOMACHEAN ETHICS
fol. 1 *Frontispiece, Book I*

This manuscript, containing Aristotle's moral treatise, the Nicomachean Ethics, was made for Andrea Matteo Acquaviva, Duke of Atri (1458–1529). The scribe is thought to be Angelos Konstantinos who wrote other manuscripts for the Duke, which are also now in Vienna. Acquaviva was himself a scholar who belonged to the humanist Accademia Pontaniana in Naples. The learned iconographic program behind the frontispieces to each of the ten books of the Ethics is probably due to him, since certain of the ideas behind it are also found in his commentary on Plutarch's *de morali virtute.*

The frontispiece to Book I shows in the center a triumphal arch decorated with classical type reliefs and statues, and in the spandrels busts of Plato, on the left, and Aristotle, on the right. In the center the female figure probably personifies Reason who ensures Happiness in the exercise of the Virtues. She is shown receiving Prudence, Fortitude, Justice and Temperance.

In the upper part of the page the Platonic doctrine of "Ideas" is represented, the Heavenly "Idea" above and its earthly representatives below. Aristotle also discusses in Book I the nature of Happiness and Solon's famous saying to Croesus, King of Lydia: "Call no man happy before his death." Two examples are illustrated, both taken from Herodotus, not from the Ethics. To the right is Croesus himself, whom Apollo rescues from the pyre to which his enemy, Cyrus of Persia, had consigned him. To the left are Cleobis and Biton. They pulled their mother to the Temple of Hera for a festival when she had no oxen. She prayed to the Goddess to grant them the greatest happiness possible for mortals as a reward, and they died in their sleep in the Temple the following night.

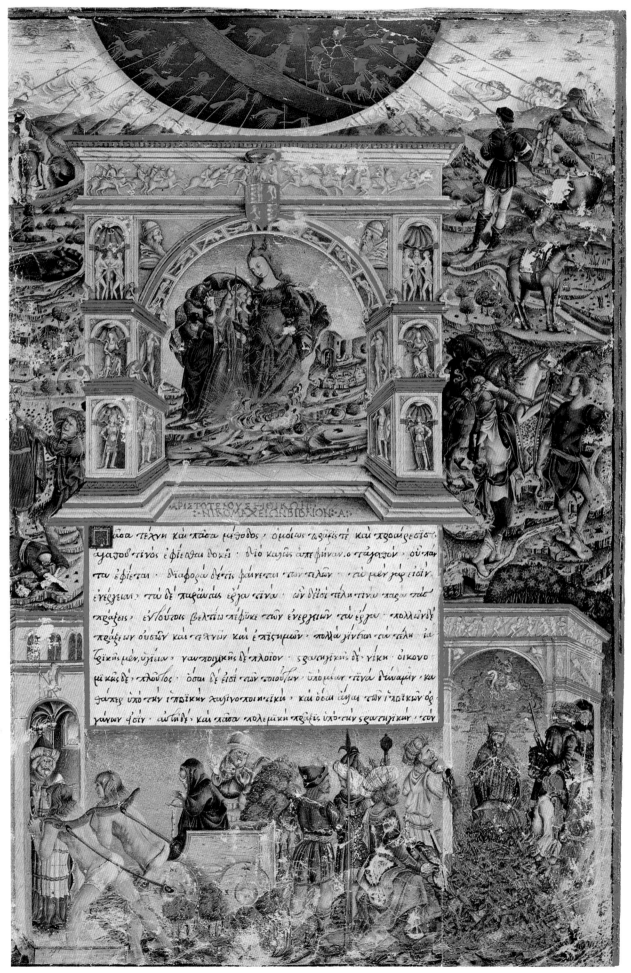

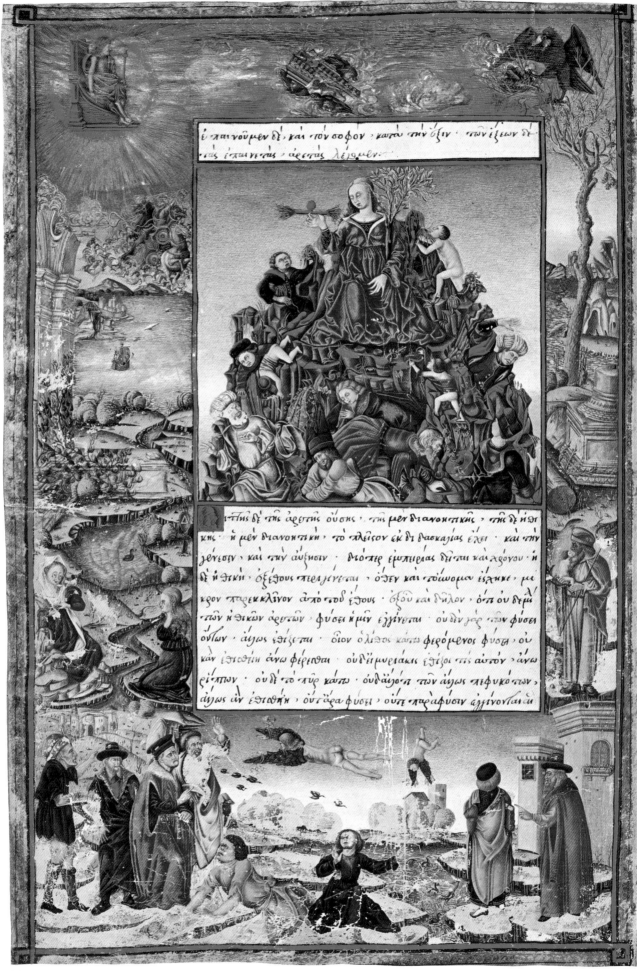

## PLATE 36

Aristotle, Nicomachean Ethics
fol. 10v *Frontispiece, Book II*

Book II is concerned with the moral virtues. Aristotle considers virtue to be a mean between two evils, excess and deficiency. The frontispiece shows an enthroned female personifying Virtue, who holds a golden apple balanced on a rod with flames at each end representing the Golden Mean. Below humans seek to climb up the mountain to attain the crown of laurel, the reward of virtue, which Virtue holds in her left hand. Most fall back in failure.

In the border are shown three mythological episodes in which Excess led to disaster. To the left, above, is the story of Phaethon's ill-fated attempt to drive the chariot of the sun and his consequent fall and destruction; below is the flight of Dedalus and his son, Icarus, who flew too near the sun so that the wax securing his wings melted and he fell; and to the right in the middle is Saturn, the father of Zeus, devouring one of his other children. Below, to the right, Aristotle points out these scenes for the edification of his pupil, Alexander the Great.

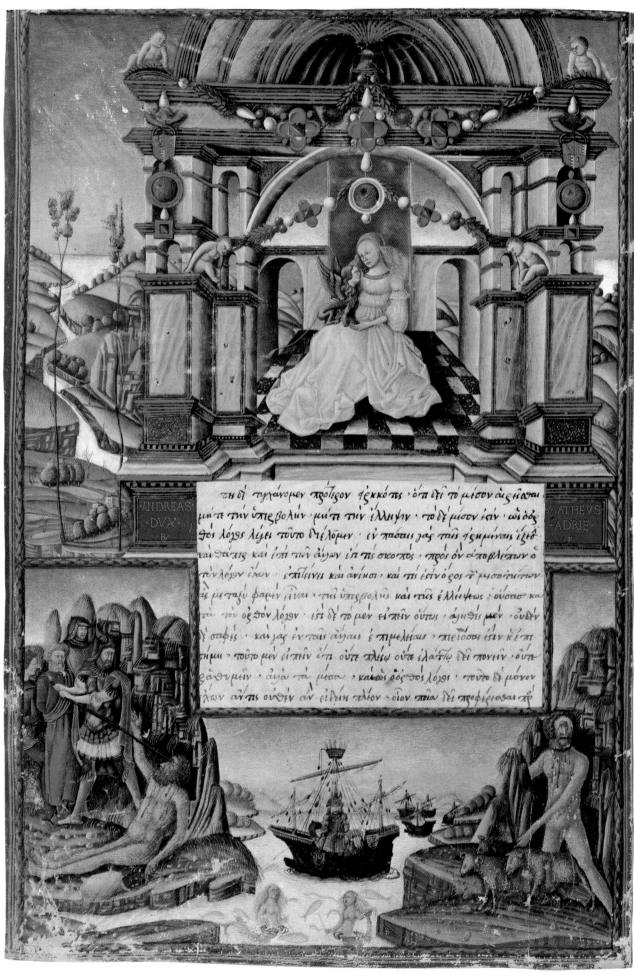

PLATE 37

ARISTOTLE, NICOMACHEAN ETHICS
fol. 45v *Frontispiece, Book VI*

This is the frontispiece to Book VI, in which Aristotle turns to the intellectual
as opposed to the moral virtues. The seated woman holding a Sphinx personifies Practical Wisdom, with whose help man can pursue the Golden Mean and
answer the riddles of the Sphinx. Below are episodes from the story of the
cunning Odysseus as a type of Practical Wisdom. On the left he blinds the
giant, Polyphemus, with a flaming torch, and on the right he escapes from
the giant's cave in which he was imprisoned, by clinging to the belly of the
giant's bellwether. In the center he is shown bound to the mast to hear the
beguiling singing of the Sirens.

On the aedicule are the arms of Acquaviva and the words: *Andreas Dux.
Matheus Adrie* and the initials *R.F.*. The latter probably stand for *Reginaldus
fecit.* On folio 80 the artist has signed his name in full: *Reginaldus Piramus
monopolitanus librum hunc picturis decoravit mirifice.* Monopoli is near Bari
and the Duke owned estates there. Reginaldus decorated other manuscripts
for the Duke, although this is the most splendid. His classicisizing style owes
much to the Paduan school. (Plates 13–14)

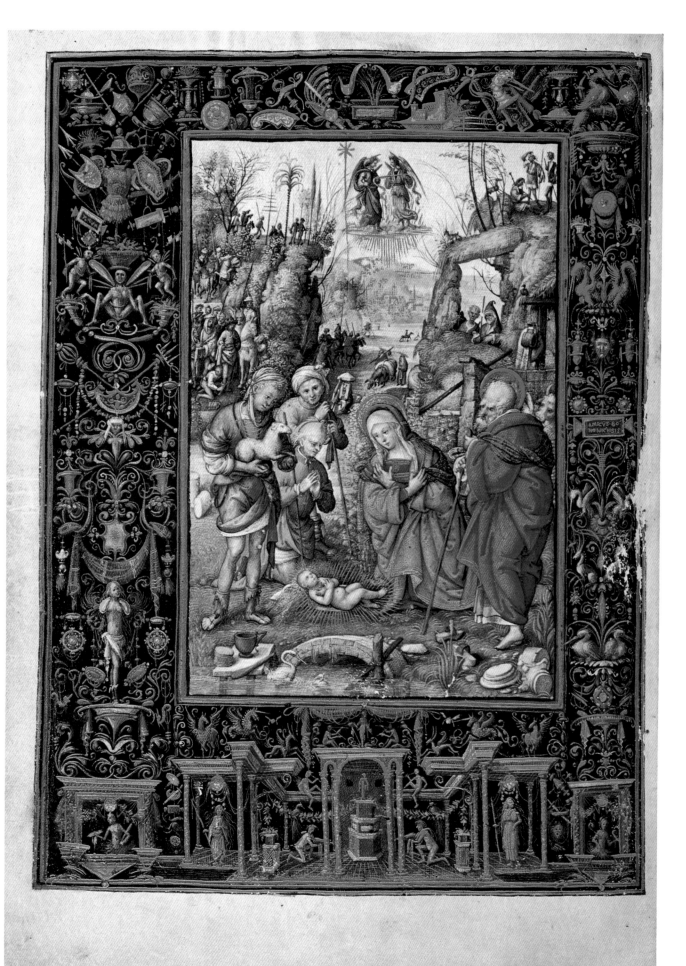

38

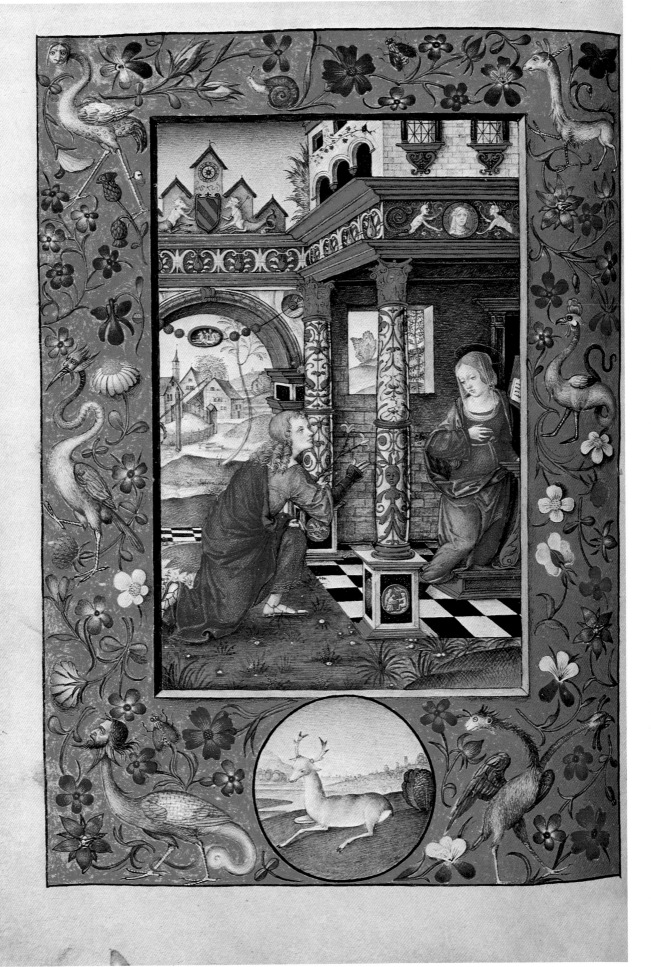

## PLATE 38

THE GHISLIERI HOURS
fol. 15v *The Adoration of the Shepherds*

This Book of Hours bears the arms and initials (*BP.GI.*) of Bonaparte
Ghislieri of Bologna, who is known to have been a senator of the city in
1522. The manuscript was written between 1492 and 1503 since there is a col-
lect for Pope Alexander VI, and the script has been attributed by Cockerell
and Wardrop to Pierantonio Sallando who worked in Bologna from 1489
until his death some time after 1540. Sallando taught grammar in the University of Bologna and later held an appointment there to teach the art of
writing.

The illumination is by three artists, of whom the first, Amico Aspertini,
signs his name on a cartouche in the right border of this page: *Amicus Bonon-
iensis*. He was born c. 1475 and died in 1552. He was a pupil of Lorenzo
Costa and his work also shows the influence of Francia and of Ercole Roberti.
Aspertini was described by a contemporary as a passionate emulator of antiquity, and three sketchbooks and numerous drawings survive in which we can
see him at work copying classical remains in Rome and elsewhere. The trophies
in the left border derive from an antique stucco copied in one of these sketchbooks, the 'Codex Wolfegg.' The border decoration of *grotteschi* belongs to
a type of decoration known to the Renaissance above all after the discovery of
the Golden House of Nero in Rome, and of which the most famous example
(in the Vatican Loggie) is by Raphael and his school.

PLATE 39

THE GHISLIERI HOURS
fol. 74v *The Annunciation*

The Annunciation shown here is by a second artist, to whom is also due the
main part of the decoration of the Hours. He is to be identified, as Mr. D. H.
Turner has already suggested, with Matteo da Milano, documented from payments in the Breviary of Duke Ercole I of Ferrara (died 1505) now at Modena.
Matteo uses borders with naturalistic flowers painted as if scattered on the
page and *trompe l'oeil* features such as the two flies on this page. Such borders
were derived from contemporary and earlier Flemish illumination and his
landscapes are also Flemish in feeling. At the same time, however, he denies
the *trompe l'oeil* effect by the insertion of grotesques, human heads, birds, etc.,
which would not appear in the realistic Flemish borders.

The third artist in the manuscript is none other than Pietro Perugino (1446–
1524), who signed the miniature of Saint Sebastian on folio 132v (not reproduced here).

The Hours was bought from Prince Albani in Rome in 1838 by James
Dennistoun, the historian of Urbino. In a description of the manuscript written
for Lord Ashburnham (Plate 3) to whom he later sold the manuscript, he
tells with smug satisfaction how the authorities in Rome made an unsuccessful
attempt to prevent the export of such an important national treasure. The Hours
was then bought by the great manuscript collector Henry Yates Thompson
(Plates 6–7), from Lord Ashburnham's son in 1897 and was bequeathed in
1941 to the British Museum by Mrs. Yates Thompson.

118

## PLATE 40

PETRARCH, CANZONIERE, TRIONFI
fol. 149v *The Triumph of Love*

Petrarch's great vernacular works, the Sonnets and the *Trionfi,* were immensely popular in the Renaissance, and numerous *de luxe* illustrated manuscripts survive containing the two works. The Sonnets inspired by his love for Laura were written in the years at Avignon from 1327, when he first saw Laura, to 1341, and the *Trionfi,* an allegorical poem on the triumph of the Divine over all worldly things, were written towards the end of his life.

The present manuscript, as a prefatory poem tells us, was written by Jacobus Lilius (Giacomo Giglio, who does not appear to be otherwise known) evidently for himself, since it bears his own arms. The name of the illuminator, Marmitta, is also given. Francesco Marmitta of Parma died in 1505. The only work so far attributed to him which is datable is the Missal given by Cardinal Domenico della Rovere to the Cathedral of Turin between 1498 and 1501. The present manuscript is likely to be of the same date or slightly later. A third manuscript illuminated by Marmitta, the Durazzo Hours in the Biblioteca Berio, Genoa, was written by Pierantonio Sallando (Plates 38–39).

The first of the *Trionfi* is the Triumph of Love, which is succeeded by the Triumphs of Chastity, Death, Fame, Time, and Eternity. The winged God of Love rides on an ornate triumphal car (Plate 32) which is drawn by four white horses and accompanied by the men and women he has enslaved. The hero Hercules with his club is prominent among them. Below two *putti* support the arms of Giglio. In the border are representations of cameos with classical figures. Vasari says that Marmitta turned from painting to *intaglio* and that he was a great imitator of ancient gems (*Vite,* ed. Milanesi, V. 1880, p. 383).

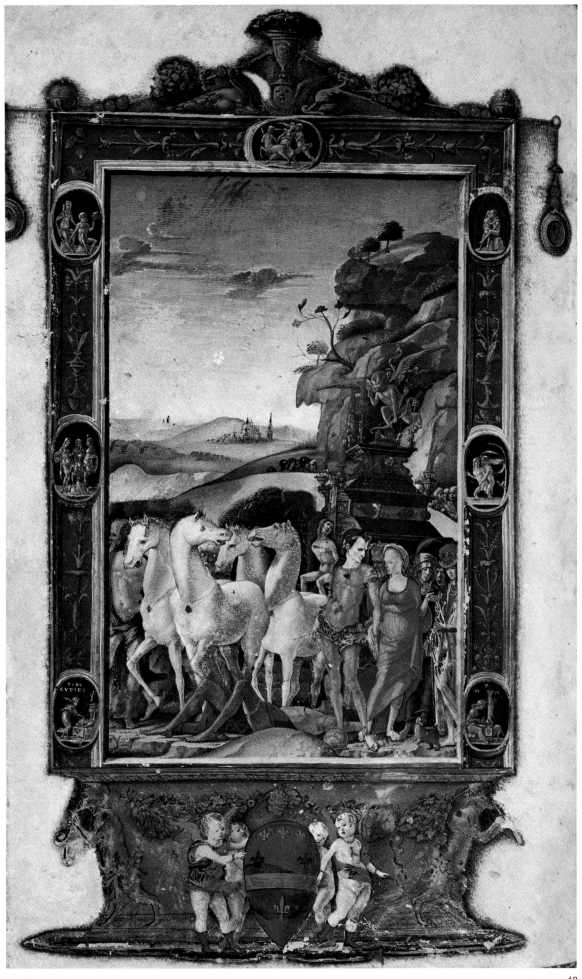